T0209858

TAKE YOUR PLACE

Understanding Righteousness:
The Doorway to Receiving All God
has Freely Given You

CHRIS BARNETT

WESTBOW
PRESS®
A DIVISION OF THOMAS NELSON
& ZONDERVAN

WestBow Press books may be ordered through booksellers or by contacting:

WestBow Press
A Division of Thomas Nelson & Zondervan
1663 Liberty Drive
Bloomington, IN 47403
www.westbowpress.com
844-714-3454

Scripture taken from the New King James Version® Copyright © 1982
by Thomas Nelson. Used by permission. All rights reserved.

Scripture taken from the King James Version of the Bible.

ISBN: 978-1-6642-4047-6 (sc)
ISBN: 978-1-6642-4048-3 (hc)
ISBN: 978-1-6642-4046-9 (e)

Library of Congress Control Number: 2021914176

Print information available on the last page.

WestBow Press rev. date: 08/05/2021

CONTENTS

DEDICATION

I want to dedicate this book, first of all, to my parents, Jim and Jannie Barnett, I want to say thank you. You raised us in the fear and admonition of the Lord. Without that, I would not be where I am today. To Dad Hagin, Pastor and Mrs. Hagin and all of my Rhema Bible Training College instructors who sowed the truth of God's Word into my life, thank you! And to all the people who will receive revelation of the truth of God's Word when reading this book, your life will never be the same. Walk in the fullness of all God has freely given you. Last but definitely not least, I dedicate this book to the Lord, may everything it accomplishes bring glory to you.

1

A Place of Righteousness

One morning I was sitting at my dining room table studying the Word of God concerning righteousness. As I studied, the Lord said to me, "Understanding righteousness is the doorway to receiving everything I have freely given you."

The Word of God says in 2 Corinthians 5:21, "For He (God) made Him (Jesus) who knew no sin to be sin for us, that we might become the righteousness of God in Him." Adam lost his place of right standing with God when he disobeyed what God told him (*see* Gen. 3), but we have been brought back into a place of right standing with God in Christ, back into a place of fellowship with Him. We could not and did not do anything to attain or earn this place. God freely gave it to us. Christ made Himself to identify with us in our sinful state and made us to identify with Him in His place of righteousness. It is up to each one of us to understand that, step into it, and walk in the fullness of all God has freely given us.

When God spoke to me in the quietness as I studied at my dining room table, I was well versed in the Bible. I'd spent three years studying the Bible and training for ministry at Rhema Bible Training College. I spent many hours sitting in different classes and countless hours reading and studying the Word of God. One of the classes at Rhema was called Righteousness. I remember sitting in that class with tears of joy flowing down my face as the Holy Spirit revealed to me the simplest of truths concerning righteousness and my place in Christ. It was so freeing! I had never experienced such freedom. It was almost overwhelming. My entire life I tried to earn God's goodness, but it was a free gift all along.

I always believed I had to reach a place of almost being perfect in order to receive anything from Him. With the understanding of righteousness, the burden of trying to "earn anything" just lifted off me. All the misconceptions of God and who I thought He was faded away. Over the last fifteen years, the Lord has taught me and brought me into a deeper understanding of who He is, of righteousness, and of our place in Christ. He didn't give me this revelation to keep to myself but to share with others. It has been a life-changing revelation for me, and I believe it will be for you as well. I remember telling Him, "Now that I know the truth and walk in this freedom, You must use me to tell the whole world, because everyone has the right to walk in these freedoms that I so much enjoy."

I am not the first or only person to receive such revelation, but this is His revelation in my words, and I know He will use it to minister to those who will listen. So I challenge you to have ears to hear, and you will receive revelation you have never received before. Through this revelation, you will be able to receive and walk in all God has freely given you. But for this revelation to come, a person must first get to know God, and in order to get to know Him, we must get into His Word. His Word gives us insight and reveals to us who He is and His nature. We must know Him and His nature before we can fully understand righteousness and what He has freely given to us.

Jesus said in His prayer in the 17th chapter of the Gospel of John that eternal life is to know the Father (John 17:3). Not knowing God has been a major problem throughout history. Most people don't believe they can know God or His nature. Many have been taught that the things of God and knowing Him are above our ability as people, that all the things of God are a mystery, and that all the things of God are above our ability to understand, but that is simply not true. In fact, the opposite is true. You can know God! All the things of God are not a mystery, and you can understand Him, but because of wrong teaching, there has been a lack of that knowledge, and people have not received all God intended them to have.

God tells us in Hosea 4:6, "My people are destroyed for lack of knowledge." So a lack of knowledge was even a problem back in those days, and it continues to be a problem today. But the Bible tells us in 2 Peter 1:3, "as His divine power has given to us all things that pertain to life and godliness, through the knowledge of Him who called us by glory and virtue." He has given us all we will ever need to live victorious lives. Romans 12:2 says, "And do not be conformed to this world, but be transformed by the renewing of your mind, that you may prove what *is* that good and acceptable and perfect will of God." Paul wrote in 1 Corinthians 2:9–10, "Eye has not seen, nor ear heard, nor have entered into the heart of man the things which God has prepared for those who love Him.' But God has revealed them to us through His Spirit." Paul also wrote in his letter to the Ephesians in chapter 5, verse 17, "Therefore do not be unwise, but understand what the will of the Lord is."

So you can see the Word clearly tells us we are expected to know God and His will for our lives. We are expected to know and walk in what He has freely given us. People all around us are dying before their time. Diseases and cancers are taking the lives of our loved ones. People are suffering from depression, anxiety, and oppression. They are being diagnosed with emotional, mental, and psychological conditions, and, sadly, they don't realize there is a cure. That is why I am writing this book. I want to see lives saved and thought processes changed, and I want to shed some light on the truths of the Word of God. I want to inspire you to get into the Bible for yourself and have a personal relationship with God, because then you will receive revelation and know what the truth is because the Spirit of God will show you.

You will enter a realm of life in Christ that is truly heavenly. The truth will set you free. You will forever be changed. You will have a joy that the situations of this world cannot take away. Depression and oppression will no longer have authority to control your lives. You will be set free from emotional and psychological conditions. You will begin to live life on this earth like God truly intended it to be. You will walk in divine health and protection. You will find financial freedom you have not experienced before.

But like I said, this can only happen when we know God and His nature; when we understand righteousness, have a solid understanding of how it is ours and what it brings. Remember, 2 Peter 1:3 says that God has given us all things that pertain unto life and godliness through the knowledge. That means He has done everything He needed to do to give us the ability to live long, healthy, prosperous, joyous lives. But because of wrong teaching, some think He is withholding these things from us until we reach a place of "deserving them." My friend, we could never reach a place of "deserving them," but because of God's grace, love, and goodness, they are ours as soon as we accept Jesus as our Lord and Savior! As believers, we are in right standing with Him and worthy of receiving all these benefits!

With that in mind, let's further look at what it means to be in right standing with God, which the Bible refers to as righteousness. The writer of Hebrews says it like this, "For we do not have a High Priest who cannot sympathize with our weaknesses, but was in all points tempted as we are, yet without sin. Let us therefore come boldly to the throne of grace, that we may obtain mercy and find grace to help in time of need" (Heb. 4:15–16).

So, to put it in our modern terminology, righteousness is the ability to stand in the presence of God without the sense of guilt or inferiority, as if sin never existed. It means we can have the confidence to walk right into His presence any time we want with no hesitation. It is vitally important we come to this place of understanding our righteousness in Christ.

In Ephesians 6, which the apostle Paul wrote from Rome, he tells us to put on the whole armor of God. One of those pieces of armor is called the breastplate of righteousness. The Roman army ruled the world at that time. They were a mighty fighting force, equipped with the best armor and weapons of the day. Paul understood this and used these pieces of armor and weapons as examples to make a point. He saw these pieces of armor firsthand and saw how effective they were in protecting the Roman soldier.

He spoke about the breastplate and how it protected the vital organs of the body from injury, especially the heart. Even God, when he formed man out of the dust of the earth, put the vital organs and the heart behind the ribs as a form of protection. The Roman breastplate was the best in the world at doing just that, protecting the heart and the vital organs. Paul used this as an example to make a point because he understood the importance of what people believed in their innermost beings—in their spirits or hearts.

He also knew that people had to understand and believe in their hearts the righteousness they have in Christ and how it was freely given to them. He understood that if people knew and believed these things in their innermost beings, it would act like a breastplate and protect against anything that was not true from penetrating their beliefs and would make receiving from God much easier.

So, as you read this book, be open to the Spirit of God showing you some things you didn't know because I believe He is going to bring revelation to you. You are going to see things like you never have before. He is literally going to change the way you think. He will reveal the truth to you, and those things that are not the truth will fade away. He will build a foundational belief in your heart that will set you on a course that will bring you into the divine destiny He laid out for you since the beginning of time.

In order to begin to understand, we cannot start halfway through the Bible. No, we must start at the beginning, because to understand righteousness, we need to know and understand God. A foundation must be built on just that—knowing God. You must get to know Him in order to trust Him. You might ask, "How can I know and understand God?" We get to know Him through His Word, and it's easier than you think. You will see. So pay close attention to what I present to you. There is a reason. Remember we are building a foundation, and there are certain things I want you to see and realize. So, let's get started. This is going to be fun!

2

First Impressions

The Bible says in Genesis 1 that God created the heavens and the earth, and it goes on to say He spent six days doing so, then on the seventh day He rested or ceased from creating. But let's look at what He did at the end of the sixth day.

Genesis 1:26–28 says, "Then God said, 'Let Us make man in Our image, according to Our likeness; let them have dominion over the fish of the sea, over the birds of the air, and over the cattle, over all the earth and over every creeping thing that creeps on the earth.' So God created man in His own image; in the image of God He created him; male and female He created them. Then God blessed them, and God said to them, 'Be fruitful and multiply; fill the earth and subdue it; have dominion over the fish of the sea, over the birds of the air, and over every living thing that moves on the earth.'"

After doing that, God planted a garden in Eden and put the man He created there (Gen. 2:8). Later in Genesis 2, it says, "And the Lord God commanded the man, saying, 'Of every tree of the garden you may freely eat; but of the tree of the knowledge of good and evil you shall not eat, for in the day that you eat of it you shall surely die'" (Gen. 2:16–17).

So God made man (Adam), and gave him authority over all the earth, to run it and manage it as we see fit. God put us in a position; He gave us a place. We did not have to do anything for it or to earn it. We were in right standing with Him, we were walking in divine health, we were taken care of, and completely safe and preserved. All these things were freely given to us. It belonged to Him, but He gave us a place in it, then He placed us in the garden.

It's very similar to a man who owns a company. He owns it, but he has a manager who runs things. In this case the earth belongs to God, but we are the managers. You could also compare it to leasing an apartment or house. It does not belong to you, but you have been given the right or authority to live there. You have the authority to use and enjoy all the things that pertain to the apartment.

It says here in the first two chapters of Genesis, that God gave the earth to Adam—leased it to him—and fully expected him to manage it and enjoy all the benefits of it. But I believe God fully intended for Adam to ask Him to advise, and for Him to have influence on how to run things at times.

Let's stop here for a second and point out a couple of things. When you are in a lease, there are certain things you are at liberty to do as the occupant, but there are also things you must get the approval of the owner before doing them. Also, by law, the owner must notify you before he can come on the premises to work or do any maintenance. You have both signed a lease or a contract, you have both given your word, and you are both bound by it. (We will talk a little bit more about this later in this book.)

So God placed Adam in the Garden of Eden and told him the rules. Then, Genesis 2:19 says, "Out of the ground the Lord God formed every beast of the field and every bird of the air, and brought them to Adam to see what he would call them. And whatever Adam called each living creature, that was its name."

So God had placed Adam in the garden to manage it and now he had dominion over all of the animals and any creeping things in the garden.

Now the Lord did not want Adam to be alone, so He made him a wife. We read later in Genesis 2, "And the Lord God caused a deep sleep to fall on Adam, and he slept; and He took one of his ribs and closed the flesh in its place. Then the rib which the Lord God had taken from man He made into a woman, and He brought her to the man. And Adam said: 'This is now bone of my bones and flesh of my flesh; she shall be called Woman, because she was taken out of Man'" (Gen. 2:21–23). Adam later named his wife Eve (Gen. 3:20).

In Genesis 3, the serpent tricked Eve, and she ate of the tree. Then she gave some to Adam and he ate as well. The Bible says that in that moment their eyes were opened, and that they knew they were naked, so they made themselves clothes out of fig leaves. Then when God came walking in the garden in the cool of the day to talk with them, they hid themselves because they were naked and afraid. God asked them, "Who told you that you were naked? Did you eat of the tree I told you not to eat of?" (Gen. 3:11).

God didn't need to ask them. He already knew. He just wanted to see what they would say. We all know that because they disobeyed God, several struggles and hardships would now come on them. God put them in the garden and gave them everything they were ever going to need. Like I said before, He had given them a place. Their responsibility was to manage the earth and fellowship with God. They were given full authority over the earth. He was going to take care of them, but when they sinned and disobeyed Him, they lost that place. He was still going to take care of them, but now it was going to be from a distance.

The Bible says God is a just God, which means justice would have to be served because of their sin. They would have to be judged for their disobedience, but God chose to separate Himself from them so that He would not have to pronounce judgment on them at that moment. You can say God delayed judgment and sentencing until a later date.

If God had not separated Himself from them, they would have died right there. Sin cannot come into the presence of God. He is pure holiness, truth, and light. Judgment would have come immediately, and death would have been final, so that is why He separated Himself from them. As you read further into the Old Testament, when God spoke to Moses, His presence was on a mountain because no one could stand in His presence and live. So Moses and the children of Israel built a tabernacle, which is a fancy way of saying "home," for God's presence. In that home was a large curtain that separated man from God's holy presence. Before sin, God was always in fellowship with man, but after man's disobedience, man took on a nature of sin, and God was always in a place separated from the people.

You will discover as you read about these things that it was because of the holiness of God that He had to keep Himself separated from the people. If man were to come into contact with God's Holiness in his sinful state, judgment would have been instantaneous. So, it was an act of mercy for Him to separate Himself from them.

Now I want you to pay attention to what happens next. It is very important and will affect your understanding of everything from this point forward. At the end of Genesis 3, the Bible says God made clothes for them and drove them out of the garden so they would not eat of the tree of life. I have heard it preached that God drove them out of the garden as a form of punishment for their disobedience, but that is simply not true. It plainly states He drove them out so they would not eat of the tree of life and live forever.

In Genesis 3:22–24 it says, "Then the Lord God said, 'Behold, the man has become like one of Us, to know good and evil. And now, lest he put out his hand and take also of the tree of life, and eat, and live forever'—therefore the Lord God sent him out of the garden of Eden to till the ground from which he was taken. So He drove out the man; and He placed cherubim at the east of the garden of Eden, and a flaming sword which turned every way, to guard the way to the tree of life."

Let me point something out for your consideration. If Adam and Eve would have eaten of the tree of life and lived forever, does that mean that they would have lived forever separated from God? Evidently so, because it says that if man would have eaten of the tree of life, he would live forever. So is it safe to say that man would have been forever separated from God, with no hope of peace, joy, contentment, good health, etc. It would have been total chaos.

Either way, the Bible says God made clothes for them and drove them out of the garden for their own good, therefore separating Himself from them. By doing this He did not render a verdict, pronounce judgment, or carry out a sentence on them. The separation is what He spoke of in Genesis 2:17 when He said, "but of the tree of the knowledge of good and evil you shall not eat, for in the day that you eat of it you shall surely die." This was not referring to physical death, because they did not fall dead. This death refers to a separation from God. It simply meant a spiritual death—being separated from God—so they did not die in their sin.

Does that sound like a Heavenly Father who was mad? No! Does that sound like a Heavenly Father who is waiting in the heavens with His big hammer to smash us if we mess up? Absolutely not! He did what a loving father would do—made clothes for them and watched out for them. The giving and merciful nature of our Heavenly Father can be seen in the very beginning. It is very important that we establish this in our hearts from the start.

I have traveled all over the United States and have even lived overseas in a third-world country. And one thing I have found to be true in every place I have been is that people have a misunderstanding of who God is. Somehow, they have the wrong impression of our loving God.

Let me ask you a question. The first time you meet someone, will their attitude, the way they talk to you, the way they treat you, or how they treat someone else have a direct and immediate effect on who you think they are as a person? Absolutely, it will!

First impressions are important. And it is safe to say that what people are told about God or how He is presented to them, will have a direct effect on who they think He really is. It will have a direct effect on what they think of His nature and character. When you get a wrong first impression, that changes what you expect from them from that point forward.

I have prayed for everyone who would read this book, and I believe the Spirit of God is ministering to you. Things are being revealed to your heart, and you are going to see things like you never have before. From this point forward as you read this book, I want you to decide in your heart to think and believe this:

God is a good and loving Father. He loves me. He is for me, not against me.

Period! No buts! Forget anything else you have been told that does not line up with this.

3

God Needs a Covenant

You might read the title of this chapter and ask yourself, "What is a covenant?" For the context of this book, I want to focus on a blood covenant.

A blood covenant is an unbreakable covenant based on blood, resulting in the absolute union of two parties in which all assets, talents, debts, and liabilities are mutually shared. This agreement of unity is worked out in carefully defined pledges and promises that each makes to the other.

A covenant, in the biblical sense, implies much more than a contract or simple agreement. A contract always has an end date, while a covenant is a permanent arrangement. Another difference is that a contract generally involves only one part of a person, such as a skill, while a covenant covers a person's total being.

To illustrate, there was a famous missionary to Africa by the name of Stanley Livingston. He was known to have covenants with several different tribes throughout his time there. When he first arrived at a particular region all his supplies were stolen, and I believe it happened more than once. Finally, one of the locals told him that he needed to make a covenant with a particular tribe. The tribe was known by all to be very big with many warriors, and they were feared by all. Stanley asked why he needed to make a covenant with them. The man told him that by making a covenant with them, the tribe would be bound to protect him from all that meant him harm. So, Stanley traveled to the region where the tribe was located and spoke with the chief. They made a covenant.

It just so happened that the chief had some stomach issues, and he discovered that the milk from the goats Stanley had with him soothed his stomach. So as part of the pledges and promises established in the covenant, Stanley gave the chief some goats that continually supplied the chief with milk for his stomach, and the chief would supply Stanley with the protection he needed as he traveled.

Stanley was presented with a tribal token as a gift. The token represented the covenant he had with this tribe. Stanley made sure the token was always visible for all to see. From that point on, when people would come to steal Stanley's supplies, they would see the token and leave immediately without stealing anything from him or doing him any harm. They knew the power of the covenant! They knew if they stole from or harmed Stanley or anyone in his party, they would face the wrath of the warrior tribe.

I want you to notice something about this covenant. He needed protection; the chief needed the milk from the goats for his stomach. They each had something that was valuable to themselves, but they also saw that what they had was also very much needed by the other party. In making a covenant, it is taking what is valuable to you and giving it to someone else because you see their need.

The lives of the warriors and the protection they provided was very important for the tribe's survival, but Stanley had a need for that protection. The chief understood that. The milk from Stanley's goats was part of the provision he brought with him for his survival in Africa, but he also saw the need the tribe had, specifically the chief, because of the relief it brought to him.

Now let's apply covenant thinking to us. Because of Adam and Eve's disobedience, they opened the door for the curse. Sickness, disease, and poverty were now part of man's everyday life, and, even worse, now man could not be in direct fellowship with God. Sin brought all these things on man; God did not do this to him. Man was on his own to take care of himself, struggling to survive, working and tilling the ground to provide for his family. Mankind needed a savior.

Adam and Eve had disobeyed God, turned their back on Him, listened to Satan who disguised himself as a serpent, and in doing so gave him the authority to speak into and influence their lives. Colossians 1:13 references that man was now in the kingdom of darkness. He was separated from God and needed a way to come back into fellowship with Him, to come back into right standing with Him.

God also needed a way back into man's life. He wanted direct fellowship with man, a relationship with each person on the earth, and to regain a place of influence in man's life. He had given authority of the earth to Adam, but had lost his influence into man's life when Adam and Eve chose to listen to Satan. He needed a legal way back to a place of influence, but He also needed to do it in such a way that He honored His Word. He needed a man who would listen to, obey, trust, and fellowship with Him, which would be giving an invitation to God to have a direct influence on his life so He could fix what man had messed up through his disobedience.

Let's look again at what the definition of a covenant is and apply it to what we just read. Remember, a blood covenant is an unbreakable covenant based on blood, resulting in the absolute union of two parties in which all assets, talents, debts, and liabilities are mutually shared. This agreement of unity is worked out in carefully defined pledges and promises that each makes to the other.

God and man each had assets and talents. Man also came with debts and liabilities. They needed each other to fulfill the plan God had for mankind. You will understand this more as you continue to read this book.

So, in this chapter, I want us to look at a couple of covenants in the Old Testament to get a better understanding. Having an understanding will simply strengthen your faith in God and make your love and understanding for Him grow.

In Genesis 6, the Bible tells us man had become evil, all his thoughts were evil, and the earth was filled with violence. This is what happens to man when God is not present in his life. Remember when I mentioned how God drove Adam out of the garden to keep him from eating of the tree of life and living forever? If God had not done so and man would have eaten of the tree of life, he would have lived in this evil and violent state forever. God needed to do something about it. He needed to bring judgment upon the earth, but because He had given the authority of the earth to man, He could not do it without the involvement of a man.

There was a man named Noah. He and his family had kept themselves from evil. They continued to walk in the fear of God and God loved them and gave them grace (Gen. 6:8). It was important to God to save him.

In Genesis 6:13, God said to Noah, "The end of all flesh has come before Me, for the earth is filled with violence through them; and behold, I will destroy them with the earth." He continued in verses 17 and 18, "And behold, I Myself am bringing floodwaters on the earth, to destroy from under heaven all flesh in which is the breath of life; everything that is on the earth shall die. But I will establish My covenant with you; and you shall go into the ark—you, your sons, your wife, and your sons' wives with you."

When Noah finished building the Ark, God told him to go inside with his family and all the animals He gathered, and God closed the door. Then God judged the wickedness in the land with a flood and destroyed all evil men from the earth. When the floodwaters receded and Noah came out of the Ark, he offered an offering to the Lord and blood was shed, as a sign of the covenant. Genesis 8:20 tells us, "Then Noah built an altar to the Lord and took of every clean animal and of every clean bird and offered burnt offerings on the altar."

You'll remember that in the previous chapter we discussed the aspects of a lease, the legalities of it, and how binding it is. With that in mind, I want you to think about this: *God gave His word to man. When He did so, He was going to keep it no matter what! Why? Because it is His nature and His character to always keep His word! He wanted man to know and He still wants man to always and forever know that when He gives His word or makes a promise, He will keep it!*

After the flood, God made another covenant, not only with man, but also with the earth and all that is alive in it and put a sign of the covenant in the sky. Genesis 9:9–17 says, "'And as for Me, behold, I establish My covenant with you and with your descendants after you, and with every living creature that is with you: the birds, the cattle, and every beast of the earth with you, of all that go out of the ark, every beast of the earth. Thus I establish My covenant with you: Never again shall all flesh be cut off by the waters of the flood; never again shall there be a flood to destroy the earth.' And God said: 'This is the sign of the covenant which I make between Me and you, and every living creature that is with you, for perpetual generations: I set My rainbow in the cloud, and it shall be for the sign of the covenant between Me and the earth. It shall be, when I bring a cloud over the earth, that the rainbow shall be seen in the cloud; and I will remember My covenant which is between Me and you and every living creature of all flesh; the waters shall never again become a flood to destroy all flesh. The rainbow shall be in the cloud, and I will look on it to remember the everlasting covenant between God and every living creature of all flesh that is on the earth.' And God said to Noah, 'This is the sign of the covenant which I have established between Me and all flesh that is on the earth.'"

I know some of you are asking, "So why are people being killed by so much rain that causes flooding when God promised He would not do that anymore?" I'd answer with some questions of my own. Did man ask God for wisdom before building the dams? Did people ask for God's wisdom before building their cities or houses close to rivers that get flooded due to heavy rain?

No, they did not. Did man ask God for wisdom before building their cities next to the oceans where storms come to land and destroy everything in its path? No, they did not! So we must not blame God when, if we would have asked Him for His wisdom, He would have told us to do things differently. Unfortunately, God gets blamed for a lot of things He had absolutely nothing to do with, but it's simply a result of man not seeking advice and wisdom from Him.

Now I want us to look at another man and a little bit of his life leading up to the making of another covenant. This is probably the most important covenant God made with man. It is the covenant that He makes with Abram, shortly thereafter to be known as Abraham. I want you to pay particular attention to the details of the different things God tells Abram He is going to do and the promises He makes to him. These promises have to do with us to this very day.

Let's start in Genesis 12. "Now the Lord had said to Abram: 'Get out of your country, from your family and from your father's house, to a land that I will show you. I will make you a great nation; I will bless you and make your name great; and you shall be a blessing. I will bless those who bless you, and I will curse him who curses you; and in you all the families of the earth shall be blessed.' So Abram departed as the Lord had spoken to him, and Lot went with him. And Abram was seventy-five years old when he departed from Haran. Then Abram took Sarai his wife and Lot his brother's son, and all their possessions that they had gathered, and the people whom they had acquired in Haran, and they departed to go to the land of Canaan. So they came to the land of Canaan. Abram passed through the land to the place of Shechem, as far as the terebinth tree of Moreh. And the Canaanites were then in the land. Then the Lord appeared to Abram and said, 'To your descendants I will give this land.' And there he built an altar to the Lord, who had appeared to him" (Gen. 12:1–7).

Then in Chapter 13 the story continues. "Then Abram went up from Egypt, he and his wife and all that he had, and Lot with him, to the South. Abram was very rich in livestock, in silver, and in gold. And he went on his journey from the South as far as Bethel, to the place where his tent had been at the beginning, between Bethel and Ai, to the place of the altar which he had made there at first. And there Abram called on the name of the Lord … And the Lord said to Abram, after Lot had separated from him: 'Lift your eyes now and look from the place where you are— northward, southward, eastward, and westward; for all the land which you see I give to you and your descendants forever. And I will make your descendants as the dust of the earth; so that if a man could number the dust of the earth, then your descendants also could be numbered. Arise, walk in the land through its length and its width, for I give it to you.' Then Abram moved his tent, and went and dwelt by the terebinth trees of Mamre, which are in Hebron, and built an altar there to the Lord."

Then we come to Chapter 14. There is something I want to point out in this chapter. I won't go into a lot of detail, but I believe it is important for us to see. God gave Abram and his servants supernatural strength and favor in a time of tribulation because Abram was faithful and obedient to Him. Much of Abram's family and their possessions had been taken by the men of several kings, and God helped him get it all back.

Genesis 14:12–17 reads, "They also took Lot, Abram's brother's son who dwelt in Sodom, and his goods, and departed. Then one who had escaped came and told Abram the Hebrew, for he dwelt by the terebinth trees of Mamre the Amorite, brother of Eshcol and brother of Aner; and they were allies with Abram. Now when Abram heard that his brother was taken captive, he armed his three hundred and eighteen trained servants who were born in his own house, and went in pursuit as far as Dan. He divided his forces against them by night, and he and his servants attacked them and pursued them as far as Hobah, which is north of Damascus. So he brought back all the goods, and also brought back his brother Lot and his goods, as well as the women and the people. And the king of Sodom went out to meet him at the Valley of Shaveh (that is, the King's Valley), after his return from the defeat of Chedorlaomer and the kings who were with him."

I put the entire fifteenth chapter here because it is vitally important. God continued to tell Abram terms of the covenant; things that He would give and do for Him. He also told him of some coming tribulation but that He would use that tribulation for Abram's advantage. Then God sealed the covenant with blood.

"After these things the word of the Lord came to Abram in a vision, saying, 'Do not be afraid, Abram. I am your shield, your exceedingly great reward.' But Abram said, 'Lord God, what will You give me, seeing I go childless, and the heir of my house is Eliezer of Damascus?' Then Abram said, 'Look, You have given me no offspring; indeed, one born in my house is my heir!' And behold, the word of the Lord came to him, saying, 'This one shall not be your heir, but one who will come from your own body shall be your heir.' Then He brought him outside and said, 'Look now toward heaven, and count the stars if you are able to number them.' And He said to him, 'So shall your descendants be.' And he believed in the Lord, and He accounted it to him for righteousness. Then He said to him, 'I am the Lord, who

Word, (which is Jesus, because Jesus is the Word made flesh), and God the Holy Spirit.

Let me explain; In the book of Exodus, God descends on Mount Sanai, and is like a smoking fiery furnace. Exodus 19:18 says, "Now Mount Sinai was completely in smoke, because the Lord descended upon it in fire. Its smoke ascended like the smoke of a furnace, and the whole mountain quaked greatly." The Smoking Furnace mentioned in Genesis 15:17 is the first person of the Godhead; God the Father.

Psalm 119:105 says, "Your word is a lamp to my feet And a light to my path." The Burning Lamp mentioned in Genesis 15:17 is the second person of the Godhead; God the Word.

So, you might be asking, where is God the Holy Spirit? We know that the Smoking Furnace is a reference to the Father, who we know is the first person of the Godhead. We see that the Burning Lamp is a reference to God the Word which in the New Testament was made flesh and is known as Jesus (John 1:14), who we know is the second person of the Godhead. You might think there is no mention of the Holy Spirit, who we know to be the third person of the Godhead, but He is there too. Let me show you.

Throughout the entire Bible, the Holy Spirit is known as the Oil, or Fresh Oil, or anointing Oil. Psalm 23:5 says, "You prepare a table before me in the presence of my enemies; You anoint my head with oil; my cup runs over." The Oil is the anointing of the Holy Spirit, which gives you the fuel, strength, and power to overcome what you might be going through.

The Oil is the fuel in the Burning Lamp that passed between the pieces of the animal. The Oil represents the Holy Spirit, which is the third person of the Godhead; God the Holy Spirit.

So, we have all three persons of the Godhead making a covenant with Abram.

Let's jump ahead to Genesis 17. Abram is now 99 years old, and God changes Abram's name to Abraham, which means father of many nations. God confirms His covenant with him, and tells Abraham that this is an everlasting covenant between him and God and all his seed after him. God called it an everlasting covenant. God also gave man a sign, or a reminder of the covenant. He told Abraham that from that day forward, all man children should be circumcised. That would be a sign or reminder of the covenant.

Think about it. Every time these men went to the bathroom, they were reminded of the covenant. That is where circumcision began.

Now Abraham's wife's name had also been changed from Sarai to Sarah, which means mother of multitudes. Abraham and Sarah had a promised child and named him Isaac. Isaac married a woman named Rebecca, and they had a son named Jacob. Then Jacob had 12 sons. Jacob's name was changed to Israel, and his 12 sons became the names of the 12 tribes of the new nation of Israel. These are the names of the 12 sons of Jacob (Israel) and are the names of the 12 tribes of Israel. They are Reuben, Judah, Gad, Issachar, Dan, Benjamin, Asher, Simeon, Levi, Naphtali, Zebulun, and Joseph.

Let me take a minute and point out something here that has to do with Abram and Sarai's name change to Abraham and Sarah. Name changes sometimes take place in the cutting of a covenant. For example, in a marriage covenant, when a man and a woman get married, it is customary for the woman's last name to be dropped, and for her to take on the man's last name. Although it does not specifically say that the woman should drop her last name and take the man's last name, it does imply the family or tribe will be known by the man's name. I am in no way implying that the woman is of less significance. All I am saying is that's the way God set it up. The man is to be the head of his family. We should not take that lightly. It is a biblical thing; a sign of the marriage covenant being made.

Unfortunately, people do not hold marriage covenants as a sacred thing anymore. All too often a marriage covenant is broken at the first sign of trouble. Marriage takes work and commitment, something many people lack these days. When a man and a woman make a marriage covenant, two individuals come together who usually have two different areas of strengths. The man is usually strong in certain areas of life, and has strengths and certain abilities, and the woman's strengths and abilities lie in different areas. That is why when God created the woman, He called her Adam's helpmate. Should I also point out that it takes a man and a woman to make a child? God equipped each gender with gifts and abilities. Together they make a complete team. They should rely on and depend on each other's strengths.

Remember when I was talking about the covenant Stanley Livingston and the warrior tribe made? Each had something valuable to offer to make a covenant. A marriage is the same way. Each has something valuable to bring into the marriage covenant that they make, making an unbreakable bond. Each party needs the strengths of the other. I've heard people say, "God doesn't need me." That is not at all true. God needs you! He needs a relationship with you. He needs your love and needs to give you His love. He also needs you to touch the world around you with His love. He needs to love them through you. He can't come down here and do it Himself. That is why He made you. He will use you to love people, and you may be the only person they ever encounter who can share the love of God with them. So, you see, we need Him, but He also desires and needs us. He needs us to multiply Him, He needs to love us and love through us. That is the covenant we have with Him. He gave us eternal life and all that it brings, and we give Him hands and feet to love people.

Making or cutting a covenant is important to God, and He has a purpose for it. He started with a man, Abraham, gave him a family, and turned his family into a nation. That nation is known by the same name today that God gave it several thousand years ago—the nation of Israel. They are God's chosen people, and if you read, God is the one who established it! He alone caused it to come to pass. He alone gave them the land, and established the boundaries of it. He told Abraham that He would bless those who bless the nation of Israel and curse those who come against them because Israel is God's chosen people, and it was through this covenant that He was going to bring a savior on the scene. That is why the devil tried so hard to destroy the nation of Israel throughout the Old Testament, and that is why the devil is still trying to destroy Israel today. That evil is also trying to come against and destroy the United States. You ask why? Because the United States was established on biblical principles, we are a Christian nation, and we, for the most part, have always blessed Israel and have been her friend. We have been the most blessed nation in the world since our birth. God will continue to bless us and watch over us if we continue to bless Israel, as well as continue being a Christian nation.

Now I want to go to chapter 18 and talk about what happened next. God saw the evilness of Sodom and Gomorrah. The cities were full of sexual perversion, homosexuality, and murder. God said they were great cities, but their sins were very grievous, so He was going to destroy them.

Genesis 18: says, "And the Lord said, 'Shall I hide from Abraham what I am doing?'" He answered that question in the following verses when He told Abraham about the judgment that was coming to those two cities. God understood the covenant He had with Abraham and knew it would not be honoring it if He were to destroy the cities without telling him. Then I want you to see how Abraham pleaded for mercy in verse 23 when He asked God if He would destroy the righteous in the city with the wicked. He then asked God if He would spare the city for the sake of 50? God said He would spare the city for the sake of 50 righteous. From there, Abraham asked God if He would spare the city for the sake of 45, then 40, then 30, then 20, and then 10, and each time God said He would spare the city for the righteous within it. The point I want to make is this, God was listening to and was in communication with Abraham the entire time and was willing to listen to Abraham and grant mercy if he could find that many righteous people. Another thing I want to point out is this, when God did judge people, or cities, or nations in the Old Testament, He did not judge the righteous with the guilty.

Remember I told you that Jacob, or Israel, had 12 sons? One of his son's names was Judah, which was the name of one of the tribes of Israel. It was through his seed, down many generations, that Jesus was born, not from the sperm or seed of Joseph, his earthly father, but conceived by the Holy Spirit in the womb of the virgin Mary, his mother. Jesus is known as the Lion of the tribe of Judah because Joseph and Mary were married and were a family. They were of the family of the Tribe of Judah.

So, it was through the everlasting covenant God made with Abraham that Jesus was born. Jesus is in Abraham's seed, down many generations, and an heir according to the promise that God made with Abraham—that promise being that in thy seed shall all the nations of the earth be blessed.

There was one more term of the covenant that had to be completed, and that was, "In your seed all the nations of the earth shall be blessed, because you have obeyed My voice" (Gen. 22:18). The Bible says that when we are born again that we are in Christ, and Galatians 3:29 adds, "And if you are Christ's, then you are Abraham's seed, and heirs according to the promise."

Earlier in the same chapter of Galatians, Paul wrote, "Christ has redeemed us from the curse of the law, having become a curse for us (for it is written, 'Cursed is everyone who hangs on a tree'), that the blessing of Abraham might come upon the Gentiles in Christ Jesus, that we might receive the promise of the Spirit through faith" (Gal. 3:13–14).

It is absolutely beautiful what God has done for us, and He did it all through a covenant. A covenant is significant in God's eyes and should not be taken lightly. The act of cutting a covenant has been around for hundreds, and in some cultures thousands, of years. There are probably times throughout your life when a covenant was being made and you were not even aware of it. For example, covenants were very sacred among the Native Americans of North America as we know it. Do you ever remember seeing a movie where a white man and a Native American made a covenant, discussed the terms of it, sometimes gifts or trade goods were exchanged, each gift or trade good being significant to the other, and then they sealed it by cutting each other's palms and then let their blood flow together? This was the cutting of a covenant and sealing it with blood. Man has been known to break an unbreakable covenant because of our weakness, but God has never broken His part of the covenant. Even when man broke his word, God never broke His. He has never failed to bring about one promise in the covenants He has made. Not one time.

So let me review and highlight some important things concerning the everlasting blood covenant God made with man. What were man's assets or talents he had to offer in making a covenant? Dominion. God did not have a legal way to move in the earth without man. Because of His Word, He had given dominion and authority of the earth to man. Man also had a body in order to move on the earth and take the love of God to the world. Women had a womb, in which a man could be born to pay for the sins of the world.

What were the debts and liabilities of man? He owed a debt for his disobedience. What were man's needs? He needed to be restored to God, but he also needed healing and to be delivered from poverty. These were assets God had readily available. God had eternal life to give, and in this eternal life was restoration to Him, healing for man's body, and deliverance from poverty. It was everything man needed to be restored to the place God had intended him to be in all along. Do you see the importance of the blood covenant? Each party gave what they could to meet each other's needs and to bring about the desired outcome for both parties.

4

Promise Made, Promise Kept

L et's jump forward several thousand years from what is known as the Old Testament to the New Testament and talk about the coming of Christ, who is also the fulfilling of the promise. It's not that the rest of the Old Testament isn't important, because it is extremely important. My purpose in writing this book was not to explain the entire Bible, which is simply impossible. My purpose for writing this book is to highlight things that will cause you to want to pick up the Bible to get to know God better, and cause you to want to have a personal relationship with Him so you can enjoy all the things He has freely given you.

In the first book of the New Testament, we find the coming of Jesus. Matthew 1:18–25 tells us, "Now the birth of Jesus Christ was as follows: After His mother Mary was betrothed to Joseph, before they came together, she was found with child of the Holy Spirit. Then Joseph her husband, being a just man, and not wanting to make her a public example, was minded to put her away secretly. But while he thought about these things, behold, an angel of the Lord appeared to him in a dream, saying, 'Joseph, son of David, do not be afraid to take to you Mary your wife, for that which is conceived in her is of the Holy Spirit. And she will bring forth a Son, and you shall call His name Jesus, for He will save His people from their sins.' So all this was done that it might be fulfilled which was spoken by the Lord through the prophet, saying: 'Behold, the virgin shall be with child, and bear a Son, and they shall call His name Immanuel,' which is translated, 'God with us.' Then Joseph, being aroused from sleep, did as the angel of the Lord commanded him and took to him his wife, and did not know her till she had brought forth her firstborn Son. And he called His name Jesus."

Notice that they were married, yet Joseph did not know her intimately. The purpose of this marriage was so that they would be a family, and Jesus would be born into a family of the Tribe of Judah.

This was Matthew's account of Jesus' birth. Matthew was one of the 12 disciples of Jesus. He had a firsthand account of all that took place. There was another disciple who was also there with Jesus throughout His entire ministry, who wrote an account of the birth of Jesus. His name was Luke. They were both with Jesus throughout the entire time of His ministry on earth. I want to bring attention to a detail in Luke, who was a physician, which Matthew, who was a tax collector, chose not to highlight. I want you to notice what the angel said to Mary when he was telling her of the coming child, and her response.

Luke 1:26–28 says, "Now in the sixth month the angel Gabriel was sent by God to a city of Galilee named Nazareth, to a virgin betrothed to a man whose name was Joseph, of the house of David. The virgin's name was Mary. And having come in, the angel said to her, 'Rejoice, highly favored one, the Lord is with you; blessed are you among women!' But when she saw him, she was troubled at his saying, and considered what manner of greeting this was. Then the angel said to her, 'Do not be afraid, Mary, for you have found favor with God. And behold, you will conceive in your womb and bring forth a Son, and shall call His name Jesus. He will be great, and will be called the Son of the Highest; and the Lord God will give Him the throne of His father David. And He will reign over the house of Jacob forever, and of His kingdom there will be no end.' Then Mary said to the angel, 'How can this be, since I do not know a man?' And the angel answered and said to her, 'The Holy Spirit will come upon you, and the power of the Highest will overshadow you; therefore, also, that Holy One who is to be born will be called the Son of God. Now indeed, Elizabeth your relative has also conceived a son in her old age; and this is now the sixth month for her who was called barren. For with God nothing will be impossible.' Then Mary said, 'Behold the maidservant of the Lord! Let it be to me according to your word.' And the angel departed from her."

Notice Mary's response in verse 38. She said, "Let it be to me according to your word." God made us, and we belong to Him, but He also gave us a free will. We have the right to accept or reject the things He has given us or wants to do through us. Adam and Eve chose to disobey, but Mary chose to accept what God wanted for her life. I do believe she could have also declined what God had for her. If she would have declined, God would have chosen another woman. God does not force anything on us. No, that would be oppressive. We are not puppets on a string. He is not

5

The God Man

In the book of John, the Bible tells us that Jesus, the Word, was born in the flesh and became flesh, born in the likeness of man. "In the beginning was the Word, and the Word was with God, and the Word was God. He was in the beginning with God. All things were made through Him, and without Him nothing was made that was made. In Him was life, and the life was the light of men. And the light shines in the darkness, and the darkness did not comprehend it … And the Word became flesh and dwelt among us, and we beheld His glory, the glory as of the only begotten of the Father, full of grace and truth" (John 1:1–5, 14).

In Paul's letter to the Philippians, he wrote, "Let this mind be in you which was also in Christ Jesus, who, being in the form of God, did not consider it robbery to be equal with God, but made Himself of no reputation, taking the form of a bondservant, and coming in the likeness of men" (Phil. 2:5–7).

It's important to understand that this was the only way it could happen. Man sinned, disobeyed God, and owed a debt for that sin. He owed his life. The life of a man is in his blood. Adam could have attempted to pay that debt, but he had a sin nature now, and his blood was unclean. But the Bible says in Hebrews 9:22 that without the shedding of blood, there is no remission of sin. Adam had sinned and taken on a sin nature. He was not pure anymore. God the Father could not pay the debt for man's sin. If He could, don't you think He would have done it in the garden when man first sinned? But He couldn't. This was a debt that man owed, and man would have to pay it. God is a just God, and justice had to be served.

God made a covenant with Abraham and sealed the covenant by which Jesus was going to be brought on the scene at the right time. I want to talk briefly about what happened in those thousands of years between the sealing of the covenant and the coming of Jesus. God did not just disappear and leave Abraham's family to fend for themselves. He was watching over them the entire time.

If you read the story, Joseph, Jacob's son and one of Abraham's great grandsons, was sold into slavery by his jealous brothers. He wound up in Egypt. Through a series of events, Joseph was made second in command to all of Egypt, under Pharaoh. There was a serious period of drought in all the land, but God used what Satan meant for harm in the bondage of Joseph and turned it around for good. He gave Joseph favor in the eyes of Pharaoh, who gave him control over all of Egypt. Joseph was able to use his position to feed his family during the drought, and all his family, including his brothers, who were the names of the tribes of Israel, survived. Over the next 400 years, they survived in Egypt and became great in number, just as God told Abraham would happen. (You can read all that took place concerning these things by reading Genesis 23 through Genesis 50.)

Now let's jump ahead a little more than 400 years. The pharaoh who showed Joseph favor died and there was a new pharaoh in charge. The children of Israel faced great bondage under the rule of the new pharaoh. God raised up a man by the name of Moses. He was born at this time and became the man God used to bring the children of Israel out of the bondage (read the book of Exodus to get the full picture). After Moses led the children of Israel out of bondage and they crossed the Red Sea, God caused Moses to establish the law. This law was what God used to teach the people right from wrong. In the book of Galatians in the New Testament, Paul calls it the schoolmaster (Gal. 3:24 KJV). The law Moses established contained 613 laws. Yes, you read that right—613!

There were 10 commandments, but 613 laws within the law of Moses. God used these commandments and statutes to keep people walking upright, doing what was right in His eyes. Nobody is perfect, so when someone did mess up in some of the, as I'll call them, minor situations, they had to perform certain rituals or cleansings to continue their life. But there were certain things that if a person messed up and broke the law, the punishment was quite severe. Then, once a year, there was a ceremony which the high priest performed. An animal was sacrificed, and blood was shed on behalf of the people. That would allow their sins to be covered. They wouldn't be forgiven, just covered. God allowed their sins to be covered and pronounced them righteous for another year. He could then continue to lead and protect them.

They had to do this every year without fail. The blood of that sacrifice would cover the sins of the people. This took place for nearly 1500 years. It was a commandment, and this is how their temporary righteousness was attained. It was through works—the performing of all these commandments and statutes—that purchased their righteousness for another year, and God could continue to preserve them. You can read all about these things in the books of Leviticus, Numbers, and Deuteronomy. It's a hard read, but I believe everyone should read it at least a couple of times to get a perspective on just what took place, as well as to get an understanding of what was expected under the Law.

It is also vitally important that you read the rest of the Old Testament, which will tell of the different periods of time for the nation of Israel, promises God made to Abraham concerning his family for generations, and how God caused them to come to pass. You'll see how He led the children of Israel in different periods of time, but allowed them to make their own choices whether to obey or go against what He was leading them to do. When they obey what He was leading them to do for their best interest, it went well for the people. In fact, "well" is an understatement. When they obeyed God, they lived abundant and supernatural lives. They had no lack or want. They literally had everything they needed.

When they did not do what God wanted them to do, they reaped the consequences of their decisions. But hear me when I say this: God did not cause the bad that came on them in these times of disobedience! He simply allowed them to make the choice and allowed it to play out. They either reaped the benefit or consequence of their choice. He also knew they would learn from their bad decisions.

There were times in my life when I would make a bad decision, and I would suffer the consequences. My dad did not always bail me out of the situation I had gotten myself into. In fact, some of the time he didn't even know about the trouble I had gotten myself into. If he had known and bailed me out every time, I never would have learned and appreciated the benefit of doing the right thing or making the wise choice. When he did not bail me out, it did not mean he did not love me. He knew that by me reaping the consequences of my bad or foolish decision, it would not be pleasant for me. In fact, it might even make life hard on me for a while. But he also understood I would learn from it, it would cause me to think twice about making a bad decision again, and I would grow from my experience.

That's what a good parent does. They protect their children, but they also make tough decisions that will allow their kids to grow and be ready for adulthood. The same was true with God and the nation of Israel. There were many years where they enjoyed seasons of prosperity, but there were also many years where they suffered greatly because of bad choices they made. The same is true today.

Many people wonder why things go the way they do in life. God is there to lead us if we will just ask and trust Him to do so, but He will not make the decision for you. If you make a sound decision, it will work out for you every time. Sometimes you will make a wise decision and, at first, it may seem like you made the wrong one, but if you just keep trusting God, He will cause things to work out for your good because you made a wise choice. When you insist on making a foolish choice even when He is trying to get you not to, He will allow you to make it, and He will allow it to play out so you reap consequences. When you realize your mistake, repent, and invite Him into the situation, He will turn everything around and cause you to come out victorious, just like He did throughout the Bible when people turned to Him for help.

Some people have the mindset that everything happens for a reason. I believe 95 percent of everything that happens in life, whether bad or good, is the result of a decision you made, and if something bad is happening in your life, it's not God doing it. Chances are it is the result of a bad choice. Some of the bad choices we make can affect our health, our finances, our families, or even our jobs, but the fault lies with us, not God. Jesus plainly states in John 10:10, "The thief does not come except to steal, and to kill, and to destroy. I have come that they may have life, and that they may have it more abundantly."

Let us go back to what we were referencing earlier, the debt man owed. How was he going to pay for it? How was he going to pay a debt he was no longer qualified to pay? I spoke about it in a previous chapter that man had taken on the nature of sin and corruption. He had nothing to offer for payment. Blood was the required payment, but his blood was impure. He had become unclean because of sin. So, every man born from the loins of a man (his sperm) and the womb of a woman, was born unclean, unworthy, and with a nature to sin. Romans 5:12 explains it like this, "Therefore, just as through one man sin entered the world, and death through sin, and thus death spread to all men, because all sinned."

So, all men who were born since Adam until the time of Christ were unclean, unworthy, and not qualified to pay the debt. Man was responsible to pay the debt, yet we were not qualified to bring ourselves back into right standing with God. There was nothing we could do on our own to accomplish this. It's what the prophet Isaiah wrote about when he said, "But we are all like an unclean thing, and all our righteousnesses are like filthy rags; we all fade as a leaf, and our iniquities, like the wind, have taken us away," (Isa. 64:6). Paul said it like this in the book of Romans, "As it is written: 'There is none righteous, no, not one,'" (Rom. 3:10).

Sin had come upon all men, and he had fallen short of the glory of God. Many people take these two scriptures out of context and try to apply them to our present state, but you can't apply these two scriptures to us now. If you read the entire chapter, Paul is describing the previous state of man and says that whether Jew or Gentile, all fall short of being in right standing with God. This is the state of man before being in Christ.

Romans 3:23 tells us, "For all have sinned and fall short of the glory of God." In Romans 6, Paul went on to say, "For the wages of sin is death, but the gift of God is eternal life in Christ Jesus our Lord," (Rom. 6:23).

How was man going to pay a debt he owed when he was not qualified to pay it? He wasn't. Jesus was going to pay the debt for us! You may be asking, "Jesus is God, so how is He going to pay it? You just said God couldn't pay the debt. Man had to."

You are correct. God couldn't pay the debt, and neither could man, but a God-man without a sin nature could! Jesus was a God-man. He was 100 percent God, and also 100 percent man. The Bible says in Philippians 2 that Jesus gave up His deity and took on the form of a man. "Let this mind be in you which was also in Christ Jesus, who, being in the form of God, did not consider it robbery to be equal with God, but made Himself of no reputation, taking the form of a bondservant, and coming in the likeness of men. And being found in appearance as a man,

He humbled Himself and became obedient to the point of death, even the death of the cross," (Phil. 2:5–8).

The word "reputation" in the verses above can also be translated as authority or power. Philippians 2:7 in the New Living Translation says it like this, "He gave up His divine privileges; He took the humble position of a slave."

Jesus Himself said it like this in John 5:26–27, "For as the Father has life in Himself, so He has granted the Son to have life in Himself, and has given Him authority to execute judgment also, because He is the Son of Man."

Notice Jesus didn't say He had been given authority to execute judgement because He was God, nor did He say it was because He was the Son of God. The reason Jesus said He was given authority to execute judgement was because He was the Son of Man. He was 100 percent God, and 100 percent man. It was because He was a flesh and blood man that He could pay the debt man owed.

So because He came from heaven, and not by the will of man or a sexual act, but by the will of the Father, conceived by the Holy Spirit, He was the Son of God. Then you also must realize that because He was born through the womb of a woman, was flesh and blood, and in the likeness of a man, He was also the Son of Man. He came to execute judgement on Himself, to stand in the place for man, and because he was the Son of Man, he was qualified. He was a God-man without power. I say a God-man without power because the Bible specifically says He gave up His authority (power). The Bible also says He had to be anointed by God with power after He was baptized by John the Baptist (Luke 4:18). Jesus was 30 years old when this anointing happened, because that was Jewish custom. It also says that afterwards Jesus changed the water into wine, which was his first miracle. So from

His birth until that point, He didn't do any miracles, healing, or deliverance. He had no power to do so. It was only after He was anointed by God as a man at the age of 30 that He received power to do these things.

The book of Acts says it like this, "That word you know, which was proclaimed throughout all Judea, and began from Galilee after the baptism which John preached: how God anointed Jesus of Nazareth with the Holy Spirit and with power, who went about doing good and healing all who were oppressed by the devil, for God was with Him" (Acts 10:37–38).

It's a beautiful thing that God did. His love for us was and is so great! It's also a beautiful thing what Jesus did. He was in heaven. He did not owe the debt for sin, but came to earth as a man so He could pay it. That is how much He loved you and me!

That reminds me of an old song we used to sing in church called "He Paid a Debt He Did Not Owe." The first verse says, "He paid a debt He did not owe. I owed a debt I could not pay. I needed someone to wash my sins away. And now I sing a brand-new song, Amazing Grace. Christ Jesus paid the debt that I could never pay."

Praise God! I am so thankful that He did!

6

Paid in Full

The Bible says Jesus gave His life. Man did not take it. Jesus laid it down. Even God didn't lay it down. It was Jesus. If you remember in Matthew 26:53, Jesus said He could call for 12 legions of angels to rescue Him when the soldiers came for Him and they would have come, but Jesus didn't ask. It was His choice to die for you and me. He saw the needs of the many outweigh the needs of the one. His asset—His life—paid another man's debt. He shared the liability of all other men and paid the debt. That is covenant talk!

It appears Jesus was also tempted to quit, because in the Garden of Gethsemane He prayed to God and basically asked if there was another way for the debt to be paid, which tells me His suffering must have been great. The Bible said He sweated great drops of blood when He was praying. This is a condition known as hematohidrosis. There are only a few documented cases of this condition. It is caused by extremely high levels of stress. It's not caused by the stress of everyday life. It's not caused by stress that comes from a job or stress we feel when raising our families.

What might cause a person to be stressed to the point of sweating blood? The knowledge of imminent death, and the knowledge that it will be slow and tortuous. If you have seen the movie, *The Passion of the Christ*, you have a good idea of what Jesus endured for you and me. But the historical writings of that period say it was much worse than the movie shows. Many writings say Jesus' face wasn't even recognizable because of the beating He endured. His blood was shed for you and me. It was His blood that He took into the holy place in Heaven and sprinkled upon the mercy seat of God for us. Remember how I mentioned earlier that once a year, the high priest would have to take the blood of the sacrifice into the holy place of the temple to cover the sins of the people for another year? The Bible tells us in Hebrews that Jesus became our High Priest and went into the holy place of heaven once with His own blood and sprinkled it on the mercy seat of heaven to obtain eternal redemption for you and me.

Hebrews 9:11–12 says, "But Christ came as High Priest of the good things to come, with the greater and more perfect tabernacle not made with hands, that is, not of this creation. Not with the blood of goats and calves, but with His own blood He entered the Most Holy Place once for all, having obtained eternal redemption."

I don't know about you, but to me that is something to shout about!!! Hallelujah!!!

The Bible also says Jesus went through, experienced, and was tempted in all points as we were yet without sin (Heb. 4:15). There is not an emotion or temptation we have experienced that He did not experience and overcome.

You see, my friend, there's nothing you or I have done or could ever do to be reconciled to God. Yet sometimes we think that because we are not walking in the blessing in a particular area of our life, it is because we have done something wrong or must do better. No! No! No! A thousand times no! It's actually just a lack of understanding of how to walk in all the blessings that are hindering you from it.

I want you to really focus on this paragraph. Read it a few times if you need to. Write it down and put it on your refrigerator. Do whatever you need to do to remember what I'm about to tell you. Your righteousness is not based on your merit. Your righteousness is only based on the redemptive work of Christ Jesus. He as a man paid your debt. You don't owe anything for your righteousness. He is not withholding anything from you. What He endured, what He went through, it was enough. There was nothing you could have done. God knew there was nothing you could ever do, so Jesus came and did it for you. Yet we sometimes think what He did was not enough, and we must do our part. No, there is nothing you could or can do. He already did it for you. It is being in Christ that gives us our righteousness.

We must renew our minds to think the way God thinks. The Bible says in 2 Corinthians 5:17–21, "Therefore, if anyone is in Christ, he is a new creation; old things have passed away; behold, all things have become new. Now all things are of God, who has reconciled us to Himself through Jesus Christ, and has given us the ministry of reconciliation, that is, that God was in Christ reconciling the world to Himself, not imputing their trespasses to them, and has committed to us the word of reconciliation. Now then, we are ambassadors for Christ, as though God were pleading through us: we implore you on Christ's behalf, be reconciled to God. For He made Him who knew no sin to be sin for us, that we might become the righteousness of God in Him."

He reconciled us to Himself. We had nothing to do with it. The only thing we had to do was accept Jesus as our Lord and Savior.

When man fell in the Garden of Eden, spiritual death, sickness, and poverty came into the world. The Bible says Jesus' blood was the payment for our sin. The punishment for the sins of the world was put on Him. In verse 21 above it says He was made to be sin, who knew no sin. He did not commit any sin. The burden of sin and the debt man owed was placed on Him as a man, and the righteousness of Jesus was given to us. We were made righteous. He identified Himself with our sinful state, and made us identify with His right standing with God. He traded places with us. The prophet Isaiah prophesied this many hundred years before Jesus was born.

We read in Isaiah 53:1–5, "Who has believed our report? And to whom has the arm of the Lord been revealed? For He shall grow up before Him as a tender plant, and as a root out of dry ground. He has no form or comeliness; and when we see Him, there is no beauty that we should desire Him. He is despised and rejected by men, a Man of sorrows and acquainted with grief. And we hid, as it were, our faces from Him; He was despised, and we did not esteem Him. Surely He has borne our griefs and carried our sorrows; yet we esteemed Him stricken, smitten by God, and afflicted. But He was wounded for our transgressions, He was bruised for our iniquities; the chastisement for our peace was upon Him, and by His stripes we are healed."

So you see, what one man lost for us, another man regained for us. And unlike the law where man's sins were covered, the blood of Christ purchased eternal redemption for us. In Christ, our sins aren't covered, but forgotten. The law required the high priest to annually offer a sacrifice for the sins of the people, but Christ became our high priest and offered one sacrifice for eternal redemption.

The Bible says we were buried with Him (Rom. 6:4). The body of sin was buried with Him, then God raised Him from the dead for our justification of the debt being paid. We were raised with Him. We are now new creations in Christ (2 Cor. 5:17). Our debt has been paid. We are to no longer identify with the man of the past who was buried with Christ, but to identify with the new man that was raised with Christ as a new creation.

We are no longer sinners, yet I hear people identify themselves as sinners. That gives them a sin consciousness, and makes them think they are not worthy of God's goodness. We must get away from sin consciousness and move over into righteous consciousness. We have been made to be the righteousness of God in Christ (2 Cor. 5:21). We are a new creation. We are worthy in Christ. There is not one place in the New Testament where born-again believers are referred to as sinners. They are referred to as saints, brethren, or Christians. That doesn't mean you will never sin again, because you will. No one is perfect, but that's why God put 1 John 1:9 in the Bible. It says, "If we confess our sins, He is faithful and just to forgive us our sins and to cleanse us from all unrighteousness.

When you sin, you commit an act of unrighteousness, but you do not lose your righteousness. Let me repeat that for the people in the back. Committing a sin doesn't cause you to lose your righteousness. You just repent of that act and move on in your righteousness. If you were to lose your righteousness with God every time you made a mistake, it would be like one of those revolving doors you used to play in as a kid. You would be in an unending circle, outside of the building and inside the building, outside and in, outside and in. Outside of righteousness and back into righteousness. Outside of righteousness and back into righteousness. And if you had to be perfect to receive anything from God, then you would constantly be giving it back when you messed up. You get when you're good and give it back when you mess up. That would be ridiculous, but that used to be my thought process, and it was mentally exhausting trying to stay perfect. Thank God that is not the way it is!

Could you imagine if that was true? Then if you died, you better hope you did in a period you were righteous, because if you lost your righteousness every time you messed up and you died before you had a chance to repent, then it would be sayonara! You'd go to hell. That is absolutely ridiculous!

Let me ask you a few questions. Can your child come to you and talk to you at any time they desire? If your child is sick, and you have medicine that would heal them, would you give it to them no matter how good or bad they were? Sure, you would! If your child needs a new pair of shoes, some clothes, or is hungry, would you provide those things for them no matter how good or bad they were acting? Sure, you would! Would you save your child from a dangerous situation no matter how good or bad they had been? Sure, you would! The Bible plainly states that you would in Matthew 7:11. Then it goes on to say that if you as parents know how to do this, God even knows how to do it better.

If we are not going to withhold anything good from our children such as food, clothes, healing, or protection, how in the world would we think God would? He is a better parent than we could ever think of being. Because of what Jesus did on the cross, the blessing of salvation belongs to you. All the things included in salvation belong to you. Salvation from whatever you need saving from belongs to you. Provision belongs to you. Healing belongs to you. Preservation of your life belongs to you.

God is always trying to get His goodness to us. The church has not been taught correctly about these things. They haven't been taught correctly about who God is and who we are in Him. It has caused man to believe he has to have a blind trust in God; to place a trust in God without knowledge of Him and who He is. It was so wonderful and freeing when I found out the truth of the Word of God and His character and nature. It used to make me mad when I would think about all those preachers who left me with all those negative beliefs. I used to think, *What a waste of precious years of my life believing those things.*

The Lord had to deal with me about it and told me to not harbor unforgiveness in my heart for these men, because that would cause the blessing to stop in my life. He told me they were only teaching what they believed to be the truth. He also pointed out it was just as much my fault if not more, because I had the Bible they were reading and preaching out of, and I could have gotten into it for myself and found out what it said. So, I had to choose to forgive, and I did.

I used to run from God because of how I believed. I failed trying to be perfect and became mentally exhausted. I became a professional sinner. I lived my life in the moment and for the moment. Drugs, alcohol, and unhealthy relationships were part of my everyday life. Something was always missing, and I was always looking for that one thing to fill the God-sized hole I had in my life. Life was no fun. Sure there were fun moments, but when the dust settled, I was still alone, empty, and hurting. I was a failure, and I felt like I was not good enough. My life had no meaning.

One day I decided I'd had enough. I was at rock bottom and going through a divorce. I tried everything I knew to do to make a good life. I had experienced all life in the world had to offer with no luck. I asked the Lord one day to save me because I knew there was a hell and did not want to go there when I died. I heard Him say, "Now watch what I do with your life."

All I can say now is "Wow!" It has been an amazing ride. I know the truth, and I am truly free, complete, nothing missing, and nothing broken. Do I have bad moments? Sure, I do. And at first, I still had bad months, but as time went by, and I read the Word and spent time with Him, my bad months changed to bad weeks. I kept believing. I kept reading and confessing the Word and walking in faith based on what the Word said. Sure I made mistakes, too many to count, but I repented and put them behind me and found my identity in Him, not in my mistakes. Before I knew it, my bad weeks became bad days, and over a period of time, my bad days have now become bad moments, and those moments only last as long as I allow them to. It does not happen that way without a daily walk with Him.

The old me and my past do not define me anymore. My identity is in Christ. The things that go on in my world around me don't affect my moods or attitude. My identity is in Christ and what He did for me. It is not based on my ability to be perfect, but my identity in Christ is based solely upon the redemptive work He did on the cross. I don't earn that blessing for my good deeds.

It already belongs to me, so I choose to receive it and walk in it. I make bad choices sometimes, and He allows them to play out and for me to reap the benefits of the choices I made. He doesn't do it to be mean. He does it because He knows I will learn a lesson from it. When I realize my mistake, I go to Him and repent for not checking with Him before making my bad choice, and He always forgives me and shows me the best way out and makes me triumph on the other side.

It is our prayer and fellowship with Him that invites Him into being a part of everything in our lives. Prayer is not begging God to move on our behalf or trying to convince Him to move on our behalf. No! Prayer is inviting God into our situation and expecting Him to move on our behalf or show us the best way to proceed. When He does, you and everyone around you will see that it was Him, and He will receive all the glory.

I like to describe my relationship with Him like this: I act and live every moment of every day as if He is right here with me. If you are hanging out with someone all day every day, wouldn't you talk to them all the time? Of course you would. So doing the same with God is normal. He loves it when we talk to Him throughout our day, and we will hear Him speak to our heart the more we speak with Him.

But the blessing doesn't just stop there. Jesus didn't only just save us from hell, but he also redeemed us from sickness and disease. Isaiah also prophesied of this, and Matthew gave an account of that prophecy in his writings. Matthew 8:16–17 says, "When evening had come, they brought to Him many who were demon-possessed. And He cast out the spirits with a word, and healed all who were sick, that it might be fulfilled which was spoken by Isaiah the prophet, saying: 'He Himself took our infirmities and bore our sicknesses.'" Peter also wrote about it in 1 Peter 2:24 when he said, "who Himself bore our sins in His own body on the tree, that we, having died to sins, might live for righteousness—by whose stripes you were healed."

I've heard many, many people say God put a sickness or disease on them to teach them a lesson. I've also heard them say that if someone dies of something such as cancer, it must have been their time or God needed them in heaven. That would be evil of God and it would mean He had a hand in their death. If this were true and He were to do that, it would also be going against His Word. I showed you earlier where Jesus Himself said, "The thief does not come except to steal, and to kill, and to destroy. I have come that they may have life, and that they may have *it* more abundantly" (John 10:10). Also, in Psalm 138 it says God magnifies His Word above His name, "I will worship toward Your holy temple, and praise Your name for Your lovingkindness and Your truth; for You have magnified Your word above all Your name."

God will absolutely not go against His Word!

Jesus also said something in the third gospel that I want to bring to your attention. Luke 13:10–17 says, "Now He was teaching in one of the synagogues on the Sabbath. And behold, there was a woman who had a spirit of infirmity eighteen years, and was bent over and could in no way raise herself up. But when Jesus saw her, He called her to Him and said to her, 'Woman, you are loosed from your infirmity.' And He laid His hands on her, and immediately she was made straight, and glorified God. But the ruler of the synagogue answered with indignation, because Jesus had healed on the Sabbath; and he said to the crowd, 'There are six days on which men ought to work; therefore come and be healed on them, and not on the Sabbath day.' The Lord then answered him and said, 'Hypocrite! Does not each one of you on the Sabbath loose his ox or donkey from the stall, and lead it away to water it? So ought not this woman, being a daughter of Abraham, whom Satan has bound—think of it—for eighteen years, be loosed from this bond on the Sabbath?' And when He said these things, all His adversaries were put to shame; and all the multitude rejoiced for all the glorious things that were done by Him."

Jesus plainly states in verse 16 that it was Satan who bound her, not God. And think about it like this: if God was causing people to get sick and Jesus was healing them, wouldn't they be working against each other? God's not schizophrenic!

Let's look at another scripture where the religious leaders accuse Jesus of casting out devils by a devil. Matthew 12:22–28 says, "Then one was brought to Him who was demon-possessed, blind and mute; and He healed him, so that the blind and mute man both spoke and saw. And all the multitudes were amazed and said, 'Could this be the Son of David?' Now when the Pharisees heard it they said, 'This fellow does not cast out demons except by Beelzebub, the ruler of the demons.' But Jesus knew their thoughts and said to them: 'Every kingdom divided against itself is brought to desolation, and every city or house divided against itself will not stand. If Satan casts out Satan, he is divided against himself. How then will his kingdom stand? And if I cast out demons by Beelzebub, by whom do your sons cast them out? Therefore, they shall be your judges. But if I cast out demons by the Spirit of God, surely the kingdom of God has come upon you.'"

Jesus plainly states that if a kingdom is working against itself, it will not stand. So, He can't put a devil in someone and then cast it out. That would be fighting against Himself, which is unbiblical. Jesus says He is doing it by the Spirit of God. God is not putting sickness and disease on people and then turning around and healing them.

The Bible also says in 1 Peter 5:8, "Your adversary the devil walks about like a roaring lion, seeking whom he may devour." Notice it doesn't say he is a lion, but that he walks around like a lion, looking for those who will allow him to devour them. If you are walking in untruth, you are someone who he would be able to devour. Your life, your family, and your children are all subject to being devoured by his evil schemes, because you don't know who is doing all these things and don't know how to fight against it. The Word of God plainly speaks of this in Hosea 4:6 which says, "My people are destroyed for lack of knowledge." It doesn't say "those in the world will be destroyed." It says "My people." This scripture is used in the same contexts I am using it. People are being destroyed by sickness and disease and dying before their time because of their lack of knowledge of God and His Word.

If you're not a Christian, you are also walking around outside of the kingdom of God and are subject to being attacked by Satan and devoured. But being born again doesn't automatically put you in a bubble and make you immune to the devil wreaking havoc in your life. Only the knowledge and revelation of who God truly is, who you are in Him, and walking and living in that knowledge can make you immune from being devoured by the devil.

Apart from sickness and disease, Jesus also redeemed us from poverty as well. The Bible tells us in 2 Corinthians 8:9, "For you know the grace of our Lord Jesus Christ, that though He was rich, yet for your sakes He became poor, that you through His poverty might become rich." Jesus gave up His place in heaven—His power, His glory, His riches—to become poor and to lead us back to a place of being rich in Him.

Philippians 4:19–20 drives this point home even more when it says, "And my God shall supply all your needs according to His riches in glory by Christ Jesus. Now to our God and Father be glory forever and ever. Amen."

My friend, it is not God's will for a Christian to walk around broke! He gave you hands, feet, and a mind to be able to work, but He also gave you the Word of God to stand on for supernatural provision. I'm not saying you will walk around rich, but I can say He wants you to walk around with all your needs met and blessings running over to bless those around you.

I said earlier, the reason why most people aren't walking in everything God has given them in Christ is because they don't have an understanding of who God is and their righteousness in Him. They are going by what they have heard, and, I hate to say it, but much of what they have heard is simply not true. They have not renewed their minds to the Word of God. They are still thinking in line with the natural mind, instead of a renewed mind that sees things from a different place.

That's why the Lord put it on my heart to write this book. He has given me deep revelation on many things. I don't know everything, but this book is something I know to be the truth, and have seen it proven in my life.

It is important to get into the Word of God and have a personal relationship with Him. Spend time in prayer. Pray and talk to the Lord as if He were sitting right next to you, because the truth is, He is sitting right next to you and is in your heart. Have confidence that He hears you. He is a personable God. He wants to fellowship with you. He wants to talk to you and reveal all these things to your heart because that's the only way you can walk in them. The more quality time you spend with Him in His Word, renewing your mind, and thinking like He thinks, the more the Word will come alive in you and the more you will learn to hear His voice.

The Word of God is alive and powerful (Heb. 4:12). It is alive, but it must come alive in you. When it comes alive in you, it will produce what it says. But don't get discouraged. It takes some time and you won't be perfect in it. That's where His grace comes in.

Now I am going to be straight with you: *you must make this a priority.* You must make spending time with God, reading His Word, and meditating on His Word a priority in your life. You must make prayer a priority in your life. That's the only way to get to know Him. It's the only way the Word is going to come alive in you. It's the only way you are going to be able to walk in all the good things He has for you.

The Bible says it is by grace through faith that all these things are yours (Eph. 2:8), but you must spend time with Him and His Word to find out what these things are. It's not the quantity of time you pray, but by the quality of time you pray. It's also not the number of people you have praying that causes God to hear and answer. All it takes is one person praying in faith. It's not by the good works you do or by the goodness in your heart that you receive anything from God. It's by your trust in knowing Him and the things He has given you in His Word. It's knowing they are yours already! You must move from a mindset of "I am trying to get," to the mindset of "I already have." Then by faith you receive them and act as if they are already manifested. He will reveal these things in your heart, and they will become real to you. You will begin to walk in the revelation you receive.

But you must decide what is more important in your life. Are the things of this world like sports or recreational activity more important to you than divine health and protection? Because the truth is, we all live busy lives in one way or another, and there is only so much time in a day. We give so much time to recreational activities, television, and the like, but we barely give God more than one and a half hours a week reading His Word and going to church. I'll say it again, you are not trying to "earn" anything by spending time doing these things I speak of. But it does take time to get the Word of God in you to the point that you believe it without question and learn how to apply it to your life, which enables you to walk in all that it says.

I am being straightforward with you; it's not going to do you or me any good if I sugarcoat the truth. Now, I'm not saying you and your kids can't enjoy activities, sports, and things, because you can and He wants you too. But He doesn't want you to enjoy those things at the expense of not knowing Him. Knowing Him and walking in everything He has given you will make all these extracurricular activities even more fun. But it's each person's choice. You can choose to be born again and have eternal life, but walk around sick, defeated, and broke, or you can grab ahold of all that eternal life in Christ has to offer.

He is not withholding anything from you. He has already given you everything you need to live a healthy, peaceable, and prosperous life in the redemptive work of Christ. But, like I mentioned earlier, most people are coming from a place of "trying to get," instead of coming from a place that "I already have." You can't earn it! It's already yours! But you must understand it, you must step into it, and you must take your place. Let me repeat the scripture again in 2 Peter 1:3. It says, "His divine power has given to us all things that pertain to life and godliness, through the knowledge of Him who called us by glory and virtue." It's all been given to you already! It's up to you to grasp it and cause it to come to pass in your life.

Paul said something very similar to Timothy, a pastor of a church who is already born again and has eternal life. First Timothy 6:12 says, "Fight the good fight of faith, lay hold on eternal life." You must take hold and don't let go. You must fight for it—fight the good fight of faith. Your mind and body will fight against you. But if you are in Christ, eternal life is yours! Heaven is yours! But the quality of life you have on earth depends upon you and your understanding of the Word and righteousness.

The amount of blessing you walk in depends on you and the amount of Word you have inside of you. Because when the Word is alive in you, you walk in the blessing of that Word. That's what Paul was saying when he said *lay hold* in 1 Timothy 6:12. The quality of life you live is up to you.

The Bible talks about the New Testament as the Living Will and Testament, but a will is not in effect until the death of the testator. Jesus was the testator. He died and made the will valid. It is now in effect. So, what do you do to find out what you are an heir to? You must read the Will, find out what was left for you, and take possession of it. You are now part of the family. You are an heir of God and a joint heir with Christ. Romans 8:14–17 tells us, "For as many as are led by the Spirit of God, these are sons of God. For you did not receive the spirit of bondage again to fear, but you received the Spirit of adoption by whom we cry out, 'Abba, Father.' The Spirit Himself bears witness with our spirit that we are children of God, and if children, then heirs—heirs of

God and joint heirs with Christ, if indeed we suffer with Him, that we may also be glorified together."

It's significant that God put these verses in the book of Romans and used the culture to bring light to a point He was making. Paul wrote that we have been given a "Spirit of adoption." What does that mean and why did He say it? There was no process for adoption in the Jewish culture, but in the Roman culture it was a beautiful thing. If a child was born naturally, you had the option of disowning a child for a variety of reasons. The relationship, therefore, was not necessarily desired by the parent, nor permanent. That was not the case, however, if a child was adopted.

In Rome, adopting a child meant the child was freely chosen by the parents and desired by the parents. It also meant the child would be a permanent part of the family because parents could not disown a child they adopted.

Any adopted child received a new identity. Any prior commitments, responsibilities and debts were erased. New rights and responsibilities were taken on. Also, in ancient Rome, the concept of inheritance was part of life, not something that began at death. The adopting parent did not have to die for the heir to enjoy assets of the family. Being adopted made someone an heir to their father, joint sharers in all his possessions and fully united to him. That's pretty amazing. But think about what that means to us as Christians. It is a constant reminder that we are fully desired, fully loved, and chosen by God. We have taken on a new identity through Christ! We were created for heaven, but *even now* we are heirs to God, and coheirs with Christ. Everything that belongs to God, belongs to you because you are joint heirs with Christ. Praise the Lord! Hallelujah!

If you are a Christian, it's time to take advantage of everything God has freely given you through the redemptive work of Christ and start walking in the truth of His Word. Live life to the fullest by walking in the wholeness of who God made you to be. It's time for you to take your place in Christ!

I was teaching at Global Harvest for Christ Bible College in Accra, Ghana, located in West Africa. Today the school is known as Rhema Bible Training College. I got my driver's license while I was there, and drove to school from the house where I was staying. The traffic was a nightmare. Cars were coming out of the different parts of the suburbs and were all headed to a main road which carried the majority of the traffic. I'm talking about thousands of cars in a square-mile radius. The problem was there were no stop signs or traffic signals on any of these dirt roads coming out of the suburbs. It was one massive flow of traffic that never stopped, and there was never a gap in it to allow you to enter the flow of traffic. The cars were bumper to bumper the majority of the time. If you were coming out of the suburbs, you couldn't get out onto the main dirt roadway that carried most of the traffic. If you sat there and waited for someone to let you in, you might sit there for half an hour. You literally had to take your place! You had to inch your car out to the line of traffic and then stick it in between two cars whether there was room or not. You had to make room. You had to take your place in the line of traffic or sit there for who knows how long before someone might let you in.

It's the same way with your Christian walk and the eternal life you have been given in Christ. You can sit there and never take advantage of all God has given you in this new life and remain the same, or you can take your place and walk in all that God has freely given you! The devil would like nothing more than for you to stay the same after becoming a Christian. You are no threat to him or his kingdom as long as you stay ignorant to the new life you have in Christ. He would have a much greater chance to influence you back into his kingdom. The devil doesn't want you to know of the divine authority and power you have been given in Christ. He does not want you to take your place in Christ. He does not want you to discover how you can put him under your feet. Because once you learn this and how to walk in it, he has no more control over your life. He also knows you will take people out of his kingdom because you know your rights and authority in Christ. He knows once you have taken your place there, there is nothing he can do about it.

If you are not a child of God and would like to be, let me tell you how so you can take advantage of the life He purchased for you on the cross and begin to enjoy the goodness of God in your life. The Bible says in Romans 10:9, "that if you confess with your mouth the Lord Jesus and believe in your heart that God has raised Him from the dead, you will be saved."

If you don't know Jesus or have never asked Him into your heart, you can right now. Pray this prayer with me.

"God in heaven, I have heard of Your great love for me, and how You sent Your Son, Jesus, to shed His blood and die as payment for my sin. Then you raised Him from the dead as a sign that my sins are forgiven. I choose by faith to believe this. I receive the gift of salvation. Come and live in my heart and teach me how to live for You. I confess with my mouth that Jesus is the Lord of my life and I will live for Him. Thank you for my salvation. In Jesus name. Amen."

7

Heart and Voice Activated

I remember my teenage years and up into my adult life, I would say or hear people say things like, "You never know what's going to happen," "I'm always broke," "I can never get ahead," or "It seems like I never have enough." I also remember hearing people say things like, "I always catch the flu," "I'm always sick," or "I always get sick this time of year." You've probably heard people say, "I'm a klutz," "I'm accident prone," or "I'm always breaking something." We were always expecting the worst. Little did I know at the time, we were activating a spiritual law in our lives. The spiritual law was this: what you believe in your heart and confess with your mouth will come to pass. Romans 8:2 says, "For the law of the Spirit of life in Christ Jesus has made me free from the law of sin and death." When Adam and Eve sinned and disobeyed God, it put us in a state of being separated from God. Living in the law of sin and death, we were subject to sickness, disease, poverty, and lack. Much of what we say lines up with that, so therefore it traps us in that mindset. It's what we believe and what we speak, therefore it is what we have. When we get born again, the Bible says in Colossians 1:13, "He has delivered us from the power of darkness and conveyed us into the kingdom of the Son of His love." We were translated out of the kingdom of darkness, which operates in the law of sin and death, and translated into the kingdom of His dear son, which operates in the law of the spirit of life in Christ Jesus. Both kingdoms are activated by what we believe and what we speak, so when we get born again we must change the way we think, what we believe, and what we speak. We cannot continue to believe and speak the way we did before we got born again, or we will continue to have the things we had in our lives before we got born again. In order to live and enjoy all the benefits of this new kingdom, we must activate and operate the laws of the spirit of life in Christ Jesus.

In the very beginning God gave us a place of dominion and authority. It was a place of walking in divine health with no sickness or disease. It was a place of prosperity and no lack. It was a place in His presence, a place of peace in fellowship with Him. Even though man sinned and lost that place, God never changed His mind. His original intentions are still His intentions. The Bible says the gifts and callings He gives are without repentance, which means He doesn't change His mind. The gifts and callings He gives us He means to give us. They are for a reason and are meant to accomplish what He intended. The position and gifts He gave man from the very beginning are still there to accomplish something. So, in this last chapter I want to explain how to walk in everything God intended you to walk in on this earth from the very beginning.

First, realize it is by God's grace you have been saved. He chose you. He had compassion and mercy on you. Salvation is a gift, not earned by anything you did, but freely given to you by Him. Ephesians 2:8–9 says, "For by grace you have been saved through faith, and that not of yourselves; it is the gift of God, not of works, lest anyone should boast."

Second, believe in your heart what He did for your salvation, confess it with your mouth, and declare Him as the Lord of your life. This is an exercise of your faith in what He did for you. Romans 10:8 tells us, "But what does it say? 'The word is near you, in your mouth and in your heart' (that is, the word of faith which we preach)." Mark 11:23 adds, "For assuredly, I say to you, whoever says to this mountain, 'Be removed and be cast into the sea,' and does not doubt in his heart, but believes that those things he says will be done, he will have whatever he says."

Decide for yourself to believe what the Word of God says no matter what your mind might be telling you or even what you might be seeing. Just take control of your thoughts and make the decision to believe what the Word of God says. Train yourself to watch your words. Make them line up with what the Word of God says. Ask the Spirit of God to help you. He will check you in your spirit. You will have a knowing that what you are getting ready to say is not what you need to say. Then He will give you a scripture that you can line your words up with and stand on. That is why it is so important to get into the Word of God so that you know it like you would know your multiplication tables in school. He can quickly bring you what you need to declare and speak.

Let me give you a personal example. I was in my first year at Rhema Bible Training College in Broken Arrow, Oklahoma. I was a little over halfway through the year. I developed a growth just inside the edge of my nose. It was growing in size and made it look like I needed to blow my nose. It was there all the time as well as for all to see. I could scratch it off, and it would stay gone for a couple of days, but it always grew back. I was embarrassed by it always being there and knew everybody could see it.

I got up one morning and looked at it in the mirror. I was upset it was there. The thought even crossed my mind of missing classes at Rhema that day so nobody would see it. At that moment the Holy Spirit spoke to me. He brought two verses in the Bible to my heart. The first was in Mark 11 where Jesus was hungry and saw the fig tree from afar off, but when He got to it there was no fruit on it. He cursed it, and the next day when He and the disciples passed back by the tree, it had dried up from the root. The disciples were amazed when they saw it, Jesus told them to have the faith of God. The second scripture was in Matthew 28:18 when Jesus told the disciples that all power on heaven and earth had been given to Him, and then He delegated that power to them.

I knew when He brought these to my heart He was telling me He had delegated to me the power to speak to this growth, and if I spoke in faith, it would dry up by the root. I took a couple of days and prayed specifically in tongues, because I knew the Word of God told me in Jude that I build myself up on my most holy faith when I pray in the Holy Ghost, or pray in tongues (Jude 20). I got up the morning I intended, walked into the bathroom, looked at the growth and said, "I command you to dry up by the roots and fall off my face in Jesus name," then I went about my day. That night it fell off and never grew back.

Third, keep believing and speaking even if you haven't seen it manifest yet. Call those things that are not as though they are

(Rom. 4:17). That is exercising your faith. Hebrews 11 tells us, "Now faith is the substance of things hoped for, the evidence of things not seen … But without faith it is impossible to please Him, for he who comes to God must believe that He is, and that He is a rewarder of those who diligently seek Him," (v. 1,6). It also says in Romans 10:17, "Faith comes by hearing and hearing by the Word of God."

As you have faith in His Word and get to know Him through His Word, your faith in Him will grow. That pleases Him.

Look at what God told Joshua in Joshua 1:8, "This Book of the Law shall not depart from your mouth, but you shall meditate in it day and night, that you may observe to do according to all that is written in it. For then you will make your way prosperous, and then you will have good success." The NIV translation of Joshua 1:8 says, "Keep this book of the law always on your lips; meditate on it day and night, so that you may be careful to do everything written in it. Then you will be prosperous and successful."

The more you read, believe, and speak the Word of God, the less you will be moved emotionally when something takes place in your life. The more you aren't moved emotionally but believe and speak the Word of God over your situation, the more you will prosper and be successful. John said it like this in 3 John 2, "I wish above all things that you may prosper and be in good health even as your soul prospers."

In your soulish realm where your reasoning lies is also where your emotions lie. Your emotions control your actions. John is saying, if you change the way you think and control your emotions, and therefore your actions or responses, it will affect your entire life. You do this by renewing your mind to the Word of God.

The Word of God also says in Hebrews 4:12 that the Word of God is living, powerful, and sharper than any two-edged sword. In Ephesians 6 when Paul talks about the armor of God, it says to take the sword of the Spirit, which is the Word of God. A sword in the natural is an offensive weapon. Men use it to destroy and kill their enemy. The Word of God is your sword of the Spirit. When you thrust it by speaking it out of your mouth, it destroys the evil spirits that are coming against you to get you into fear and defeat, and it will cause sickness and disease to flee from you. When you speak the Word of God, your ears hear it, and when you act on what you hear, faith comes.

Speaking the Word of God also positively charges the atmosphere around you and causes your spirit to be stirred up within you. It causes your faith to rise, as well as confidence and joy to rise within you. It also invites and directs the Spirit of God to move on your behalf in your situation.

You must meditate on the Word of God daily, and declare what God says about you and what He is to you every day. It will cause the Word of God to come alive in you, and when the Word comes alive in you, it will manifest itself in and to you. Remember, you are moving from a mindset of "trying to get," to a mindset of "I already have." Whatever you are meditating on, believing, and speaking out your mouth will manifest in your life.

What you choose to believe in your heart and speak out of your mouth is a sign of your faith. If you are speaking the Word over a particular area of your life and expecting it to happen, He will become the Lord of your life in that area. So it is important to get a better understanding of what Lord of your life means, and the depth of it. In doing so, you will better understand what He wants to be to and for you, and the greater influence you can give Him over your whole life. As your knowledge grows, your confession of His lordship over that part of your life will be evident.

I hear people all the time say, "Thank you, Lord," "Praise the Lord," or even "He is the King of kings and Lord of lords," but I don't think they understand the extent of what they are saying. I doubt they understand the depth of His lordship, and what He wants to be lord of in their lives. I don't believe the average person does.

Have they given Him lordship over every area of their lives? If they don't understand what He has made Himself lord over and apply that to their lives, they aren't confessing His lordship over those areas of their lives and therefore aren't receiving all He is for them. They aren't expressing their faith and aren't expecting anything. Remember this: His lordship over all parts of your life is heart and voice activated.

Let's take a minute to read what the Word of God says concerning His lordship.

- In Genesis 22:8, God is known as Jehovah-Jireh, which means "the Lord my Provider." The Lord provided a ram for Abraham to sacrifice on the altar in the place of his son.

So you must train yourself to speak words that line up with God being the Lord your Provider. You can use verses like Philippians 4:19 which says "And my God shall supply all your need according to His riches in glory by Christ Jesus." You have to come against any thought that you are not going to have enough. You must expect and speak that your needs will be met, whether they be financial or some other need. Refuse to speak any negative words of doubt concerning your needs. God might open a door for you to work overtime at your job or some other door that will help meet your needs. Be sure to not put Him in a box, because He may meet your needs in a way you were not expecting. I confess Him as Jehovah Jireh in my life, and He never fails to meet my needs. You must acquaint yourself with all the stories in the Bible where God met the needs of those who trusted Him, and meditate on those provisions. And listen to the Holy Spirit. He will give you the story or scripture to meditate on throughout your day.

- In Exodus 15:26, He is known as Jehovah-Rapha, which means "the Lord my Healer."

Your words must not be that He *will* heal you. The Bible says that by His stripes you were healed (1 Pet. 2:24). "Were" is past tense, so if you *were* healed when He took the stripes on His back, then you *are still* healed. Your words must be that He has already healed you, and you must believe and meditate on that constantly. Speak that over and over until there is no doubt in your heart that you are healed. Read and meditate on the places in the Bible where everyone who came to Jesus received their healing. Unbelief was the only thing that kept people from receiving their healing. I am consistently reading Psalm 91 and personalizing it. I say, "I dwell in the secret place of the Most High. I abide under the shadow of the Almighty. I say of the Lord, 'He is my refuge, my fortress, my God, in Him I trust.'" I continue on where it says no sickness, disease, or plague can come near my body or my dwelling. I also meditate on, personalize, and confess the benefits I have in Christ that are listed in Psalms 103:1–5, "Bless the Lord, O my soul; and all that is within me, bless His holy name! Bless the Lord, O my soul, and forget not all His benefits: Who forgives all your iniquities, Who heals all your diseases, Who redeems your life from destruction, Who crowns you with lovingkindness and tender mercies, Who satisfies your mouth with good things, So that your youth is renewed like the eagle's." I expect to walk in divine health and I do. Not because of anything I have done, but because of what He did for me.

- In Psalm 23:1, and John 10:11, 15, He is known as Jehovah-Raah, which means "the Lord my Shepherd." You must be confident in His ability to lead you as a shepherd would lead his flock. He will lead you to places in the Word of God to meditate on and study to prepare for something that might be coming your way. His leading will help you overcome. He will keep you well grounded in His Word and will protect you as a shepherd would protect His flock.

- In Isaiah 53:5, He is known as Jehovah-Shalom, which means "the Lord my Peace." Isaiah 26:3 tells us that God will keep him in perfect peace whose mind is fixed on Him.

  When life happens, and it will, it will try to stress you out and get you worried. Just turn your thoughts to Him; meditate on His love, His goodness, and His mercy.

Choose to put a song in your heart and worship Him. Before you know it, the thing that was bothering you will just pass away. I like to put it like this: have you ever come to a speed bump in the road that was so big you had to come to a complete stop before slowly rolling over it so it wouldn't break something on your car or send your head flying into the roof of the car? Life will treat you that way if you allow it. The devil wants you to continue to think about the life situation that is causing you so much stress. He knows if you do that you will start to speak words of doubt and fear that open the door to wreak havoc in your life. Have you ever come to a speed bump in the road that had very little rise to it at all? In fact, you didn't even have to slow down to go over it. That's the way life will be if instead of thinking about the situation, you turn your thoughts to the Lord, meditate on His goodness, sing, and rejoice. The situation won't even slow you down. It will be like that little speed bump. You noticed it, but just kept moving forward.

- In Jeremiah 23:6, He is known as Jehovah-Tsidkenu, which means "the Lord my Righteousness." The words you speak must be, "My identity is in Him, not in me or the situation." When you feel inadequate, you have to remain focused on the fact that your righteousness is based on the redemptive work of Christ, not on your merit or how righteous you may or may not feel at the time.
- In Ezekiel 48:35 and Ephesians 2:13, He is known as Jehovah-Shammah, which means "the Lord is there." Your words must be, "He is with me everywhere and always." Be confident in the indwelling of the Holy Spirit,

that He is part of every second of your life, and is there to help you in every situation that may arise.

- In Colossians 2:15, He is known as Jehovah-Nissi, which means "the Lord my Banner of Victory." Your words must be, "Whatever I go through, He will cause me to win every time, because the Word of God tells me He always causes me to triumph in Christ Jesus (2 Cor. 2:14). When something comes against me, my words and my attitude is that I will win when I come out the other side of the situation." Expect to win!

I was in a court battle years ago. In the natural, it looked as if I would lose for sure. My lawyer even told me to prepare to lose, but I told him I wouldn't lose this court battle. The Lord told me several years prior what He was going to do, and He did it. I knew no one could take away from me what God had given. I held fast to my beliefs and my confession of what I believed was going to happen. I refused to entertain the thought of losing. The thought would come, but every time it did, I cast the thought down and thought on things like, "The Lord gave, and the devil cannot take it away." I won the court battle. The judge ruled in my favor. The Lord is my Banner of Victory. He is my Jehovah-Nissi!

I'm not saying your words must be exactly what I said in any of these instances. What I am saying is that no matter what you say or how you say it, it must agree with what the Word of God says. It cannot go against it. When your words line up with the Word of God, you are operating in the law of the Spirit of Life in Christ.

Most people say Jesus is the Lord of their lives. What they are actually saying is He is Lord in their salvation, but it stops there. They don't understand He intends for His lordship to cover every area of their lives. The Bible specifically teaches that God is a detailed God. He is a God of order. He is organized. So it is safe to say that if He points things out in detail and explains things in the details like He does, there must be a reason.

He can only be Lord over what we know, what we believe in our heart, and what we confess with our mouth. By doing that, it shows you understand His will and provision for that area of your life. That invites Him into that part of your life and gives Him the authority to work in those areas. It's the expression of your faith and what you are expecting.

Faith moves God into your situation. The problem is most people believe knowing the will of God and what to expect is like a Vegas craps game. In Vegas, you never know what the dice are going to turn up. The will of God is not that way. He is specific in telling us His entire will for our lives. We have to be acquainted with His will for us, then believe and confess it. Let me give you a couple of examples to think about.

God told Noah to build an Ark and why.

God told Abraham to leave his family and why.

God told Abraham that his seed was going to inherit a land before they ever did.

God told Abraham to sacrifice Isaac on the altar, and Abraham was not afraid because God told him it was through Isaac and his seed that all the promises would come. Abraham was confident that if he sacrificed Isaac, God would raise him from the dead in order to fulfill what He told him. That is why Abraham told his servants before they walked up the mountain that he and the boy would return (Gen. 22:5).

When the children of Israel crossed over into the promised land and were beginning to take the land, God told them what to do before every battle to make it turn out in their favor. Throughout the Old Testament, God told the men of God what to do before doing it, and they just did what they were told, because they already knew what the outcome would be.

God has always revealed His will to man. He's always told them what to expect and the way things would turn out when they did things the way He told them. Not once did God tell them to do something a certain way and it did not turn out the way He said it would. God spoke through His prophets the coming of the Messiah, and He came. It was always up to man to ask and find out God's will before acting, and when they did, they were *always* victorious. When they did not, things didn't turn out well for them at all.

He has always been the Lord my Provider to those who trust Him to do so in their lives and confess it.

He has always been the Lord my Healer to those who trust Him to be so in their lives and confess it.

He has always been the Lord my Shepherd to those who trust Him to do so in their lives and confess it.

He has always been the Lord my Peace to those who trust Him to be so in their lives and confess it.

He has always been the Lord my Righteousness to those who trust that He is in their lives and confess it.

He has always been the Lord is Here to those who believe that He is in their lives and confess it.

He has always been the Lord my Banner of Victory to those who believe that He is in their lives and confess it.

Their words always lined up with what they believed and expected. What they believed and confessed was an expression of their faith. And it always came to pass. What they believed and confessed, made Him Lord over that area of their lives. They were not saying, "He *will be* this to me." They were saying "He *is* this to me."

Think about all the stories of the Old Testament. God tells us in the book of Hebrews, these are examples to us of His faithfulness (Heb. 11). Take some time and read them. Ask yourself, "What did they believe, and what did they confess? What were the words that came out of their mouths?" It was always victory or success, because God told them what would happen. They just aligned their words with what He said. They did not speak lack. They did not speak sickness. They did not speak defeat. Those who did, didn't get what God had for them.

Let me give you an example. In Numbers 13, God told Moses to send out 12 spies to spy out the Promised Land that He had already told them He was going to give to them (v.1–2). The 10 who came back and gave a report of doubt wandered in the desert for 40 years until they were dead. The two who confessed a positive report based on what they knew God told them got to enter the Promised Land and reap all the blessings God told them was theirs.

In Proverbs 18:21, the Bible says, "Death and life are in the power of the tongue, and those who love it will eat its fruit." Proverbs 6:2 tells us, "You are snared by the words of your mouth; you are taken by the words of your mouth." A snare traps an animal so the animal can only go as far as the snare allows.

Similarly, you are trapped by the words you speak. You can only have what the words you speak out of your mouth say you can have. You cannot speak lack and be prosperous. You cannot speak sickness and live in divine health. You cannot speak fear, and live in safety and peace. You cannot speak doubt and have success.

Everyone who knew the will of God and acted on it in the Old Testament came out victorious in every situation. In the New Testament, everyone who heard of Jesus, what He taught, came to Him expecting, and spoke along those lines, they received what they came for.

It was football season 2010. My son Dillon was playing for the local high school. I received a call one evening from his coach. While they were practicing certain drills, my son was seriously injured and in major pain. I took him to the ER and they admitted him. They ran some tests and found he had a grade-5 shattered spleen, and his kidneys and liver were damaged. When they put him in a room, I took him by the hand and prayed. I knew it was the will of God for him to be healed, so I just prayed a simple prayer. I commanded his body to be healed. I spoke to his spleen and commanded the bleeding to stop and his organs to be healed in Jesus name. I knew from that point the healing power of God was working in his body performing a healing. I began to thank God for his healing. Throughout the night and the next few days I would say, "The healing power of God is working in my son's body and he is healed." Even when it didn't look like anything was happening, and my mind started to think thoughts of unbelief, I continued with my confessions of faith.

The Bible says in 2 Corinthians 10:4–5, "For the weapons of our warfare are not carnal but mighty in God for the pulling down strongholds, casting down arguments and every high thing that exalts itself against the knowledge of God, bringing every thought into captivity to the obedience of Christ." When thoughts of unbelief and doubt tried to rise up, I shut them down and lined my words up with what the Word says. I continued to speak words of faith and healing over him and sang praises to God for two or three days. He was injured on a Friday, but he walked out of the hospital on Wednesday of the next week, just five days after being seriously injured. He was in church on Sunday. Praise God! It was an awesome testimony of God's faithfulness to His Word.

In Mark 6, we find some people who did not believe Jesus, but doubted what He was saying. They didn't receive anything from Him. But it wasn't because Jesus didn't want to heal them. The Bible is specific when it says that Jesus could therefore do no mighty works because of their unbelief (Mark 6:5). It doesn't say that He *would* not. It says He *could* not. God is limited on what He can do for you by what you believe and what you speak. He is constantly trying to lead us into knowing the truth, so that our beliefs line up with His will. He knows then that our words will line up with what we believe.

I want to share a saying with you. I don't know who said it, but I believe it is fitting to put it here.

What you hear determines what you think.

What you think determines what you believe.

What you believe determines what you speak.

What you speak determines what you do.

What you do determines your habits.

Your habits determine your character.

Your character determines your destiny.

Your destiny determines your legacy.

Notice the first sentence and the last sentence, I can sum it all up by saying this. What you allow yourself to hear repetitively will ultimately have an affect on your legacy, whether it be good or bad. Whether it be the truth of God's Word, music, movies, books, or even your friends and family. If the words you hear are wholesome and full of life and glorify God, they will produce a good legacy. If what you hear and listen to does not glorify God, is not wholesome, and does not contain words of life, it will produce a bad legacy. Why? Because what you allow yourself to hear, will determine what you believe. What you believe will ultimately determine what you speak, and what you speak, you will have in your life.

God says it like this in Proverbs 4:23, "Keep thy heart with all diligence, for out of it are the issues of life" (KJV).

It is the confidence in knowing the will of God for your life and what belongs to you, asking Him for it, and believing and confessing that it is yours, that brings results. The Bible says in Mark 11:23, "For assuredly, I say to you, whoever says to this mountain, 'Be removed and be cast into the sea,' and does not doubt in his heart, but believes that those things he says will be done, he will have whatever he says." Notice the word "believe" is only used once but the word "says" is used three times.

Once you believe, you must continually speak what you believe, and it will come to pass. You must be in faith, and the only way to be in faith is to know the answer before it comes. The Bible says in Romans 10:17 that faith comes by hearing and hearing by the Word of God. I like to say it like this, "Faith comes by hearing the Word of God, because His Word reveals what His will is and then you can stand on His Word, confess it, and have faith that it will come to pass."

Everyone throughout the Bible who stood in faith knew what to expect because God already told them, so they knew where to put their faith. First John 5:14–15 says, "Now this is the confidence that we have in Him, that if we ask anything according to His will, He hears us. And if we know that He hears us, whatever we ask, we know that we have the petitions that we have asked of Him."

I don't remember what year exactly it was, my son Dillon was 11 or 12 years old and had a sharp pain in the joint of his hip. I took him to the ER and they admitted him. They said he developed an abscess in the joint of his hip. They were going to keep him for a couple of days and treat it. They were trying to start an IV in his arm to administer some medicine but the nurses were having trouble getting the IV started because they could not find his vein. Two or three nurses tried a couple of times each, but failed and by this time my son was screaming and crying. I was holding his other hand trying to keep him calm, and a scripture just rose up within me. It was Matthew 18:19 which says, "Again I say to you that if two of you agree on earth concerning anything that they ask, it will be done for them by My Father in heaven." So I said to Dillon, "Hey son, agree with me according to Matthew 18:19 that the next nurse who comes in and tries to find your vein with the IV needle will find it on her first attempt. He said "Yes, I agree." I said, "Okay then. It is done." Another nurse came in, saw my son and the shape he was in and said to him, "Dillon, everything is gonna be okay." She got the needle, walked over to him and without hesitation stuck his vein the first time. She said, "There you go. I got it." A look of relief came to his face. He and I looked at each other and I said, "Praise God! Thank you, Lord."

If you ask anything according to His will which He has revealed in His Word, you know He heard you and you can have confidence that He will give you your petition (1 John 5:14–15). It is important that you read the Old and New testaments. Everything you read are examples and instructions for you. When you read them, expect Him to do the same for you. Believe that He will and has done it for you, and line your words up with what His Word says, it is a guarantee it will come to pass in your life.

Let me give you some final thoughts.

I lived in Arizona in 2005, I drove a school bus on the San Carlos Apache Reservation to pick up the little kindergartners every day. I was driving to work one morning from Globe, Arizona, where I lived. It was about 6:45, and I had just entered the reservation. I heard the Lord say, "Just like in the beginning when the Spirit of the Lord was moving upon the face of the waters, My Spirit is moving upon this nation! Speak life to it!" I almost ran off the road! The anointing came on me really strongly. I began to weep, partly because of the anointing (because at times that's what happens to me when the anointing comes on me), and partly because He was speaking at that moment to my heart and giving me revelation of what I had been hearing preached and what I had been studying. It was one of the most powerful revelations I had ever received up to then. When the Spirit of God was moving on the face of the waters, the word moving is also translated as "hovering, fluttering, or waiting in place." Then the Bible said, "God said!" The Spirit of God was waiting to hear a command from God, and when the command was given, the Spirit of God did it.

God placed mankind in the garden of Eden and gave us authority and dominion over it. How do you take your authority over something? By speaking! He always intended for man to exercise his authority over the earth by speaking and declaring the will of God, and when we did, the Spirit of God was waiting to do what we spoke. I don't believe man ever lost that authority and dominion, but we allowed ourselves to be influenced by Satan. He put evil things in our hearts, caused us to be moved emotionally, and caused us to speak what he wanted in the earth, and it came to pass.

The earth has continually regressed since that day in the garden. Even though it has been the evil spirit behind man, man has spoken and declared all that has come to pass. There are some born-again Christians who don't know the Bible says we have been taken out of the kingdom of darkness and translated into the kingdom of His dear Son (Col. 1:13), and they continue to speak as if they never left the kingdom of darkness. They have not renewed their minds to think and speak what God says. They are Christians, yet they speak lack, sickness, disease, and doubt, and that's what they have in their lives. They have been given authority so they have what they say.

When you come into the kingdom of God, renew your mind, and begin to speak with the authority God has given you from the beginning, *things will change*. The Spirit of God is just waiting for the Word of God to come out of your mouth so He can perform them and cause them to come to pass in your life. That's why the Bible says to be renewed in the spirit and attitude of your mind (Eph. 4:23), so you will speak kingdom words. You will begin to think like God thinks and develop the mind of Christ. You will speak what God's Word says about you, and you will have what you say.

To take it even further, when God said, "Let us make man in our image and let him have dominion" (Gen. 1:26), the atoms and molecules heard Him. All of creation heard Him. There have been studies done all over the world on the power of a person's words towards a plant, a piece of fruit, or food. It has even been proven how words influence a person's body, as well as their mind. They have also shown that how a child turns out when he or she grows up will be determined by the words they heard spoken over them at home.

Your words affect the world around you. A child's mind and body are affected by what they hear. You must watch the words you speak about or over your children. No matter if they hear you or not. No matter how minor or insignificant you think your words are. They hold the power to create what you speak. Have you ever walked into a room where people were arguing or fighting and felt tension in the atmosphere? The particles in the air were negatively charged. You have also probably walked into a room where people were praising God and you could just feel the love in the air. The words that come out of your mouth influence the particles in the air! God Himself gave you this authority and dominion to rule, and creation heard and knows it. So you must train yourself to speak kingdom words—words of good health, prosperity, life, and safety—so that you reign in this life.

Romans 5:17 says, "For if by the one man's offense death reigned through the one, much more those who receive abundance of grace and of the gift of righteousness will reign in life through the One, Jesus Christ." We are supposed to reign in this life and live victoriously. Jesus didn't die on the cross for us to be defeated, to live in poverty and lack, and to live in sickness and disease.

We have been crucified with Christ, raised with Christ, and we sit at the right hand of God in Christ! We sit in a place of authority and dominion. Jesus had to be raised and go to Heaven to sit down at the Father's right hand so the Holy Ghost could come and be with us, in us, and teach us how to live this life in victory. God gave us the power of attorney to act and speak on His behalf. He made us ambassadors of Christ. We are here to speak the will of the Father over the earth and our lives with the full backing of Heaven.

If you are a father, I want you to listen to me. Fathers in the Old Testament spoke blessings over their children. You have the authority to speak a blessing over your children. I continually speak the Word of God over my children and my grandchildren. I say, "My children and grandchildren are established in righteousness and great is their peace. They are taught in the ways of the Lord and they are mighty men and women of God."

Everything you speak and declare over your wife and family will come to pass. God made you the head over the family. You must speak the will of God over your family, your house, your car, your grandchildren, your animals, the trees and plants in your yard, and so much more! Your words carry the power in heaven and on earth to keep them healthy, alive, and safe.

I planted a garden this year with tomatoes, squash, cucumbers, carrots, radishes, onion, okra, corn, and watermelon. I planted everything around the third week in March. We had a very late cold spell, and even though I covered the tomato plants with five gallon buckets, I failed to get a couple of them sealed down against the ground. The cold air got into those two, and the next day when I removed the buckets from them, they were frost burned and withered up. It made me mad. If you have ever eaten a homegrown fresh tomato off of one of your vines, you know that it's amazing. You don't get that taste when you buy one in a supermarket. Having fresh tomatoes was the main reason why I even planted a garden. Like I said, it made me mad that I hadn't gotten the two buckets sealed against the ground. I immediately said, "Oh no you don't!" I stooped down and touched the two plants and said, "You will live and not die and you will produce much fruit." Over the next couple of days, I would touch them again and say, "You will not die and you will produce much fruit." I also spoke many fruit-producing words over the rest of my garden. I've been eating delicious onions and radishes up to now, and everything else is looking good. I can't wait to enjoy the vegetables that they will produce. Those two tomato plants I mentioned have come alive, are healthy looking again, and I am expecting to eat many delicious tomatoes from their branches.

Speak over every situation in your life. Speak the Word over every situation you come up against. The Word says there is death, and there is life, but to choose life (Deut. 30:19)! It's not by your might or your power that all these good things will come to pass, but it's by the Spirit of the Living God. He is listening to your words and is anxious to perform them when they line up with the will of God and the will of God is the Word of God.

Get into the Word of God and find out His will for you. Read and meditate on all the examples of God's faithfulness throughout the Bible. Start speaking life in every situation in your life and the lives of your family. Be faithful in doing this. It's not that you are trying to earn the favor of God. It is that you are trying to change the way you think and what you expect of God.

Speak only positive things about your situations and family. Declare who the Bible says you are and what the Bible says belongs to you. It probably took you a long time to develop the negative thought patterns and words you have been believing and speaking over your life, so know it is going to take some time to turn that around and change the way you think and speak. But don't lose hope. God is with you every step of the way! You are in partnership with Him. He is helping you think and speak right because only then can he cause things to be the way He intended. He cannot go against what you believe and speak. What you believe and speak is where your faith will be. Faith invites God to move in your situation by His Spirit. Take your place and be all that He has made you to be.

I cannot say this enough—you must meditate on the Word of God daily, declare what God says about you every day, and declare what He is to you. Stop in your busy life and spend some quality time talking to Him. Have a relationship with Him. It will cause the Word of God to come alive in you, and when the Word comes alive in you, it will manifest itself in and to you. Whatever you are meditating on, believing, and speaking out your mouth will manifest itself in your life.

As you read the stories throughout the Old Testament of all the mighty men and women of God, you will see that all they did was take their place in life God had given them. Throughout the New Testament, you will find out the same thing, men and women of God took their place when God showed them what He had for them to do. It was a wonderful life for them all. And I bet if you could ask them right now they would tell you they wouldn't change a thing. Thank God they did because they are examples to us to follow.

Thank God, Jesus found Himself and the will of the Father for His life in Luke 4:18–21 and said, "This day is this scripture fulfilled." Jesus took His place.

Mary the mother of Jesus heard the angel tell her the will of God for her life and said, "Let it be to me according to your word" (Luke 1:38). Mary took her place.

God declared His will for your life in His Word through the redemptive work of Christ on the cross. Find yourself in the Word and take your place!

Printed in the United States
by Baker & Taylor Publisher Services